RUSTIC FURNITURE

RUSTIC FURNITURE

Sue Honaker Stephenson

cop. a

VNR **VAN NOSTRAND REINHOLD COMPANY**
New York Cincinnati Toronto London Melbourne

To Barbara and Morrie

Printed in the United States of America

Design by Loudan Enterprises
Photography by Aubrey M. Wiley, Lynchburg, Virginia
Drawings by Anne Warner and the author

Published in 1979 by Van Nostrand Reinhold Company
A division of Litton Educational Publishing, Inc.
135 West 50th Street, New York, NY 10020, U.S.A.

Van Nostrand Reinhold Limited
1410 Birchmount Road
Scarborough, Ontario M1P 2E7, Canada

Van Nostrand Reinhold Australia Pty. Ltd.
17 Queen Street
Mitcham, Victoria 3132, Australia

Van Nostrand Reinhold Company Limited
Molly Millars Lane
Wokingham, Berkshire, England

16 15 14 13 12 11 10 9 8 7 6 5 4 3 2 1

Library of Congress Cataloging in Publication Data
Stephenson, Sue H
  Rustic furniture.
  Bibliography: p.
  Includes index.
  1. Furniture—England.   2. Decoration and
ornament, Rustic—England.   3. Furniture—United States.
4. Decoration and ornament, Rustic—United States.
I. Title.
NK2528.S73   717   78-9872
ISBN 0-442-27974-4

Contents

To the Reader

This book began as a review of rustic garden furniture in the United States and as a brief technological manual. As the accretion of interesting historical facts about the furniture grew, it became necessary to examine its origins in depth. With every step backward in time, the research consistently revealed that the furniture was intimately connected with religion and morality and with nature magic and that it was heavily freighted with multiple layers of meaning. Because the furniture seems to be finding some valid expression in the current world of fashion, I have decided to include some material on its European origins. An entire volume would be required to put all of the leaves back on the eighteenth-century trees from which rustic furniture was made, and it may be that such a volume will be forthcoming at some future time. For now, however, I should like to warn the reader that this book has been organized along "Gothic" lines; it is held together with only a slender, serpentine thread of thought—namely, that beneath the superimposition of all other manners and style upon the English nation and her offspring, America, there is a "Goth" struggling to get out.

Preface

Rus in Urbe

Long before the Roman poet Martial coined the phrase, *rus in urbe*—the country in the town—in the days of Nero's crowded, noisy Rome, rusticity had served as a marker for back-to-Nature movements. One of the longest-running fixed duels in the world is that between urbanity and rusticity. The socially polished, worldly, smart Urbanus lords it over the simple, unaffected, narrow Rusticus. Rusticus is usually portrayed as the loser—except, of course, in folk literature—but only because Urbanus uses satire as his weapon of choice and satire always proceeds from a position of superiority.

Why do these two antagonists continue to oppose each other? Possibly because they represent two halves of a whole. They need one another. In the course of man's struggle to civilize himself, his inventiveness periodically surpasses his ability to understand the consequences of his achievements. It is an old rule of history that whenever man makes a discovery, it always takes him about seventy years to decide what to do with it. When Urbanus becomes frightened of his own progress, he turns for reassurance to his more conservative and more slowly developing alter ego, Rusticus. Urbanus regulates his life by means of sand in an hourglass or gears in a clock. Rusticus submits his life to the rhythm of the natural world, and to adherence to tradition. Urbanus is like an ambitious child climbing a large tree. Having reached a certain lofty height, he goes proudly far out on a high limb; the limb sways under his weight. The child then notices how very far above the ground he has managed to climb. Thoroughly shaken, he scrambles back to the solid safety of the tree trunk. The Greeks had a term for this sort of ambition—*hubris*. It seems to be a built-in feature of *homo sapiens*, a kind of original sin, and Urbanus atones for it about once every century by taking up the tending of sheep in some idealized, bucolic setting—greatly to the amusement of Rusticus, who mistakenly assumes that he

has won a point. Not at all. After some few years of dalliance in rural Arcadia, Urbanus packs up a part of Nature and takes it back to the city with him. In the past, these objects of Nature have been presented in the diverse forms of lyric poetry, music, landscape painting, carved ornament, unclassified items of flora and fauna, public parks, golf courses, and even cemeteries.

Behold the naturalistic trophies in the suitcases of the late-twentieth-century Urbanus: rustic furniture! Ignored for fifty years, rustic furniture has returned to give the still-lingering city dweller the stylish sense of having paid a visit to Nature. This time, rustic chairs have been placed in the parlor, amid green foliage, hanging flowerpots, and rustic basketware. If the floors of the contemporary home were not so flimsy, there we should expect to see craggy rocks as well.

It happens occasionally that the investigation of a forgotten, almost insignificant artifact of craftsmanship can reveal a wealth of information about the lifestyles and mental attitudes that lie beneath the surface of larger and more complex movements of history. Rustic garden seats made their first appearance in Europe in the middle of the eighteenth century. The fashion died down at the end of that century, peaked again in the early Victorian period and also in the Edwardian era, disappeared once more during the second and third quarters of the twentieth century, and, at length, surfaced again at the beginning of the fourth quarter of this century—indoors.

The undulations of fashion in this particular style of furniture and architecture tell us a great deal about the social framework in which it found a footing. The common theme that runs through all four periods when this naturalistic decoration flourished is "Back to Nature." As a decorative symbol, a rustic seat is astonishingly literal, being constructed frequently of the bare roots of trees.

Although a certain skill in artistic perception is required to construct a rustic seat, very little else is needed. This fact takes on special significance when we consider that several of the most popular designers and cabinetmakers of the eighteenth century lent their skills to this craft: Matthew Darly, William and John Halfpenny, Thomas Chippendale, and Robert Manwaring, among others. In addition, between 1820 and 1850, many popular architects in England and America employed extensive rustic work in their fashionable designs for domestic architecture. The term *rustic* is used here to mean any artifact that is made up chiefly of unhewn parts of trees.

It seems likely that the homely rustic work has always served to express the decorative symbolism of some form of rebellion against the excesses of civilization. It is not possible to discuss the rustic style without also considering its social setting. Just as architecture is incomplete without its furniture, so is furniture incomprehensible apart from its social and spatial context. It should be said, since we are dealing here with furniture and architecture, that the house and its environs are regarded as "self" by both women and men; therefore, when we examine the artifacts of the homes and gardens of the past we study the most intimate lives of people.

The main sources used for the background social history will be found marked with an asterisk in the Bibliography. The necessary historical byways lead down some extremely interesting paths, especially in the unfamiliar territory of the nineteenth century, and although many of these excursions are beyond the scope of this book, they are well worth pursuing. In the periodicals, the personal letters and journals, the stylebooks, and the published works of the eighteenth and nineteenth centuries lies a wealth of information about the opinions and attitudes of the people who made expressive use of the curious form of furniture studied in this book. The impact of reading their own words is worth a thousand pages of secondhand description.

Because rustic work had its earliest beginnings in America in the southern Appalachian Mountains and remained a continuous craft there (at least until the beginning of World War II), I have chosen to concentrate on this region of the United States. A great deal of the source material concerning summer resorting in the Appalachian Mountains is to be found only in the various local historical society libraries containing old photographs, drawings, newspapers, letters, and published local history. Victorian studio photography has provided a valuable dating source for the furniture styles because photographers frequently used rustic furniture as studio props.

Rustic work was widely dispersed throughout Europe from 1750 onward, and it was broadly scattered in America by the end of the nineteenth century. As more of the furniture is discovered, it will be interesting to observe the variation in expressive form that it has taken in different regions.

Finally, it is important to realize that the charm of rustic work lies mostly in the eye of the urban beholder; it has seldom had anything to do with *real* rusticity. The rustic style is part of an urban fantasy. If the anthropological truth were known, we should probably find that the third generation of the first village dwellers returned to their ancestors' caves to spend their summer holidays.

Introduction

A Matter of Style

Rustic furniture and summerhouse architecture were a significant part of the fanciful scenery of the eighteenth-century English landscape garden. In order to understand the sudden appearance of rustic work in the 1750s, it is necessary to examine an esthetic revolution that began in England in the first decade of the century and then spread to the Continent. The movement seems to have occupied every important man and woman of letters, from Addison to Goethe, throughout the century. The battleground of the revolution was interior and exterior decoration.

The immediate background for this rebellion in taste and style goes back to the long reign (1643–1715) of Louis XIV. During his reign, France exercised military, political, and social dominance over most of Europe. Dominion, power, and control were rolled into one succinct statement: *"L'État c'est moi."* This absolute power, so closely identified with that of ancient Greece and Rome, stamped all of France, and a great part of Europe, with an exaggerated baroque classicism. Imperial Rome marched across the face of Europe with the Sun King and his armies, his court, his diplomats, and his train of camp followers. Solemnity, grandeur, pompous majesty spoke French while French intellectuals continued to read Greek and Latin in search of a fundamental ethos that would serve as a basis for life under this powerful monarch. At his death, the deliverance from his heavy-handed despotism resulted in an explosion into hedonistic freedom. Under both the regent Duke of Orleans and Louis XV, the formality and the constraining etiquette of the old court were abandoned. The court was dispersed from Versailles to the salons of Paris. It was a time of extravagant epicureanism that was brilliant, scintillating, and wildly irregular. Enter the style known as rococo—exotic, light, eccentric in content and line, exquisite at times, frivolous at others, and unsurpassed in elegance. It was an imaginative style that expressed totally the spirit of the age.

The French classic influence invaded England with the Restoration, the return of Charles II to the throne in 1660. If seventeenth-century England had been burdened with civil wars and a morbid brand of Protestantism, the late seventeenth and the eighteenth centuries were no less afflicted by a pious, even servile, reverence for the order, decorum, and the values of Renaissance classicism. Perhaps the most dramatic way of explaining the effects of this style upon English society is to remind ourselves that well-bred early eighteenth-century ladies and gentlemen were not allowed to laugh, merely to smile. Nor were they permitted to enjoy the dramas of Shakespeare—the French Academy had dismissed the noble bard as a barbarian poet, guilty of violating Aristotle's sacred dramatic unities. The English nation, however, was not constituted to endure such tyranny for long.

> When mighty Roast Beef was the *Englishman's* Food,
> It enobled our Veins and enriched our Blood,
> Our Soldiers were brave and our Courtiers were good.
>   Oh the Roast Beef of *Old England*,
>   And *Old English* Roast Beef.
>
> But since we have learn'd from all-conquering *France*
> To eat their Ragouts as well as to dance,
> We are fed up with nothing but vain Complaisance.
>   Oh the Roast Beef, &c.
>   —Richard Leveridge, *The British Musical Miscellany*, iii (1735).

Three new styles, the rococo, the Chinese, and the neo-Gothic, all of which were visible by the 1730s in England, were used in the decorative arts as foils to combat the classic. The preromantic rebellion in England was not directed against the values of ancient Greece and Rome so much as it expressed opposition to the rigidity of the neoclassicists, who attempted to freeze the spirit of the classic into hidebound regulations.

The psychology of style, as a formal study, has yet to be written, although nearly all estheticians recognize that the periodicity of certain styles is full of meaning. If we could reduce the matter to its bare bones, we would find a regularly occurring pendulum swing between two extremes: On the one side, man views himself as controlling or mastering his physical environment (the classical view); on the other, he sees himself either cooperating with, or being controlled by Nature (the romantic position). The classical periods are marked by regularity and restraint of the emotions and by a high level of intellectual control, whereas the romantic eras show a predilection for the irregular, the exotic, and a strong emotionalism.

It is in the periods of transition between the extremes that the line of the pendulum swing is most observable. The eighteenth century is such a transitional period. This energetic age stands between an age devoted to classical Greek and Roman ideals and one of unrestrained emotionalism. It contains as well a number of smaller oscillations between the two poles. The ground is like shifting sand, stable in one area for a short time only, and yet the overall movement of eighteenth-century style in Europe is from the gentle, but classical ideals of Shaftesbury early in the century to the passions of Rousseau toward its end.

In general, it is the artists in a given period who perceive and express the driving impulses of the age. In the eighteenth century, however, the educated classes possessed such a high level of artistic sensibility that they were competent to express themselves—and they did so, in literature ranging from essays to letters to the editors of the newly invented periodicals and newspapers. Men and women also expressed themselves in two minor art forms just then gaining recognition: landscape architecture and interior decoration. It sometimes appears that everyone who could put pen to paper (or engrave a copper plate) expressed himself or herself volubly upon the subject of style, or "taste," its nature and its effects upon the individual and the public. Moreover, many of these writers were in a position to put their theories into practice, usually in the form of designs for their own homes and gardens and their furnishings. In America, Thomas Jefferson is the outstanding example of such a man.

As the social and philosophical ideals moved away from the intellectual classicism of the court and the upper classes and toward middle-class sentiment, both the French and the English aristocracy aided and abetted the movement for a time—that is, until they realized that their own style of existence was threatened. At that point, a backlash in the form of a revival of neoclassicism (nurtured by the discoveries of the ruins of Herculaneum and Pompeii) was introduced in the 1760s.

During the second and third quarters of the eighteenth century, an exotic taste for Chinese art developed; *Chinoiserie* prevailed as a favorite ornamental decorating scheme. As a design influence, Chinoiserie had a brief, but very intense, life, as we shall see later. When the neoclassicism of the late eighteenth century arrived, Chinoiserie disappeared from the scene. It was recognized for what it had always been: the bearer in disguise of preromantic style trends, the moral enemy in the classicists' camp.

That the arts of China were selected to commingle with the rococo in replacing the massive pomposity of the Romanized Hellenic styles was no accident. Not only were the arts and crafts of China conveniently present, but also ancient Chinese civilization was a parallel development to the Hellenic culture and, therefore, a suitable source of inspiration for the decorative arts that unconsciously were meant to express opposition to the classical influence. Perhaps it would be more accurate to say that the European interpretation of the Hellenic was opposed by the European interpretation of Chinese art and thought; both were derivative styles. The fact that Europeans had an imperfect understanding of Chinese culture made it even more serviceable as a vehicle for artistic projection. Europeans freely distorted Chinese art to suit their own purposes.

In this very distortion of another culture's art lies one of the secrets of style. Ornamental style is a symbolic screen that both expresses and conceals fundamental changes occurring in social and intellectual attitudes in a given period—attitudes that would meet with massive resistance if one were fully aware of them. Style, as a means of becoming adjusted to new attitudes, is a highly successful device because of its seductiveness. Being "in style" satisfies some very primitive human needs, chiefly that of approval. Unconcealed ostentation draws forth feelings of shame in our culture, but if the adult need for approval is suitably concealed beneath an attractive and socially expressive veneer of style, it becomes acceptable.

Trapped between warring critics, the English aristocrat of the mid-eighteenth century solved his style dilemma by putting a little of everything in the garden of his estate—a Roman temple here, a Gothic ruin there, and a Chinese pagoda behind a clump of trees. Similarly, Chippendale's chair designs incorporate Chinese, Gothic, and rococo elements with impunity. The appearance of Gothic design in the 1740s is another instance of design symbolism. In general, the "Gothick Taste" represents the reemergence of British nationalism. When it first appears, it is merely superimposed as ornament upon an original classical form, as was the Chinese. The fact that the Gothic, the Chinese, and the rococo were frequently mixed tells us that the three styles had a common leitmotif; otherwise, the disparities among them would have produced a marked awareness of disunity. (As a certain sophistication developed in the 1760s, the disparities *were* sometimes remarked upon.)

We shall continue to see that rebellion, change, and style are uniquely related. The second half of the eighteenth century and the early nineteenth century rebelled against the empty formal decorum and the heavy rationalism of neoclassicism, the late nineteenth century rebelled against the rigidity of the Victorian era, and the third quarter of the twentieth century rebelled against the "classical" monoliths of government, industry, and science. On each of these occasions, Western culture returned to Nature and rustic furniture provided a symbolic lap.

PART I

The Garden and the Grotesque as Metaphor

Sixteenth-century hell gate from Bomarzo, the Park of Monsters,
in Viterbo, Italy.

CHAPTER 1

The Eighteenth Century

The English Landscape Garden

The European revolt against the ordered formality of French cultural domination begins with landscape architecture in England early in the eighteenth century. Weary of the precisely laid out, symmetrical patterns of the older Dutch and French gardens and attracted to the somewhat overgrown late Renaissance gardens of Italy, wealthy Englishmen began to design new gardens that followed the natural contours of the land. Streams were encouraged to meander, trees to grow where they appeared to have found a natural setting, and forest footpaths were added that "twisted and twirled," as Horace Walpole wrote of Alexander Pope's garden in Twickenham. Most importantly, Englishmen tore down the walls that had confined the older formal gardens. The horizontal vista opened to admit Nature. Substituted for the garden wall was a clever device known as a *ha-ha!*—a ditch that served to protect the garden area near the house from cattle and sheep. With nothing to obstruct the eye, the view from the house extended beyond the foreground to include the agricultural areas of the estate and on into the distance.

By the 1740s, many of these new gardens had been created on English estates and the new landscape movement was well on its way. Vast amounts of energy, ink, and money were poured into the remolding of the estate parks. From the beginning, the parks contained small temples and structures for shelter, which became ever more numerous and various in style. The early "conceits" and "follies" included classical temples and statuary, emblematic of specific moral associations. In many cases, written inscriptions, or "divine mottoes," served to identify a particular viewpoint. These literal guideposts, chiseled into stone seats, upon the bases of urns and statues, or over temple doorways, are reminiscent of the "checks" and "goads" carved into the limestone Mound of Purgatory in *The Divine Comedy*, and, in fact, they served approximately the same purpose. The gardens included grottoes and hermitages and deliberately constructed ruins (some of them *painted* on canvas) similar to those found in the popular Italian landscape paintings of Salvator Rosa, Claude Lorrain, and Nicolas and Gaspar Poussin, which English visitors to the Continent acquired like picture postcards. The architectural embellishments helped to create in the gardens the somber mood of the paintings; the gardens were "picturesque"—like, or suitable for, a picture.

The evolution of the English landscape garden in the eighteenth century is one of the most complex movements in European intellectual history. There were few areas of English life among the upper and middle classes that the gardens did not touch directly or indirectly. Poets, painters, architects, and philosophers; kings, queens, ladies, and gentlemen; middle-class tradesmen and professional people; and commoner gardeners and laborers participated in a colossal expression of esthetic and moral identity that was visibly displayed over the emerald acres of Britain. We have it on good evidence from every literate pen in England that the gardens served an ethical purpose, especially during the first half of the century. The fact that they were built by men of wealth for the personal aggrandizement of the owner's vanity in no way contradicts the underlying meaning; many churches have been built for the same reason. The parks and gardens were horizontal Gothic cathedrals. These secular estate parks served England as a means of institutionalizing cultural ideals and moral values. They provided a spiritual locus for an intense activity of the English conscience. From the point of view of providing lasting sustenance for the English soul, the parks were unsuccessful institutions, and in the early nineteenth century, the nation dusted off its vertical Gothic cathedral churches, restored them, built new ones, and returned to worship in them. Nonetheless, between the religious and political wars of the seventeenth century and the revival of "Abbey Gothic" in the 1820s and 1830s, England passed through a vast cycle of "melancholia and mania," nearly all of which was worked out in the symbolic realm of the natural garden or in Nature proper.

It would appear that England made use of the foreign ideals and style of Renaissance classicism as a means of surviving the political and religious upheaval engendered by the events in the seventeenth century. Classicism is fundamentally a system of control, regulation, and stability. It allows for growth and change, but at a rather carefully measured pace. Historically, the Northern European races have been impatient with the slow emotional pace of classicism and its emphasis upon standardization and group uniformity. The Northern races moved quickly and as independent individuals controlled only by loyalty to family, tribe, and an admired leader. The Northern cultures, compared with the Mediterranean, were, therefore, more fragmented and individualistic and also more comfortable with the "irrational."

Nowhere can these basic differences between barbarians and Greeks be seen more graphically than in the eighteenth-century gardens of England. Looking only at the outline forms of the estate parks, as they might have been viewed from the air, we can observe the gardens as they alter shape during the century. They begin with a classical, symmetrical plan arranged on a ninety-degree axis, carefully framed with walls. Beds of flowers or colored earth form distinct, regular, and fairly small patterns. Slowly the shapes change. Walls are removed; the land area increases in size to cover several hundred acres; many straight paths and axial avenues become crooked; rectangular canals change into ponds with jagged, irregular outlines. Untrimmed boxwood and yews grow shaggy; miniature buildings in many different styles crop up.

By the 1760s, the remaining regularity in the outlines of boundary ha-ha's!, fences, streams, and wooded areas has been effectively broken up with zigzag lines and gentle serpentine curves so that the various garden areas in the parks blend and melt into one another. Shaggy trees and shrubs serve to blur distinct lines.

The complexity in the arrangement and in the natural, luxuriant growth of the trees and plants prevents the immediate intellectual perception of an organized plan or pattern in the park, and yet the viewer *feels* that there is, somewhere in all of this complexity, a very definite, purposive pattern. It is at this very moment, in the mid-eighteenth-century garden, that the Englishman has spoken with his native voice. The visual effect is not unlike that of a page of illuminated drawing from the *Book of Kells*. Nor is it unlike the rich, contrasting emotional affects aroused by the plays of Shakespeare, which England was learning to admire once again. Aristotelian ideals of unity are not applicable to this kind of art because it refuses to recognize the confines of formal boundaries.

The Serpentine Line

In 1753, the painter William Hogarth published a treatise on esthetics, *The Analysis of Beauty*, in which he promoted the waving, serpentine line as the one true "line of beauty." Although he was not the first to do so, Hogarth gave expression in this work to the real opposition of his age to classicism: a fundamental antagonism to the mentality of the ninety-degree angle. His serpentine line had variety, intricacy, and motion. Although probably not fully aware of it, Hogarth also identified another style characteristic that always accompanies romantic eras: the love of intricacy. The waving line stimulated the imagination by disappearing from sight and then reappearing. (This is a perfect description of basketwork and it helps to explain the immense popularity in the eighteenth century of Chinese fretwork, which is basically the abstraction of basketweaving patterns worked out with rigid, joined bamboo and carved wood, the traditional building materials of the Orient. In the nineteenth and the twentieth centuries, basketwork containers and chairs mark dramatically the eras of romantic taste.)

Edmund Burke took up Hogarth's waving line and used it to declare outright war on symmetry. The landscape designers William Kent and Lancelot "Capability" Brown were advocates of the serpentine. William Kent's "Nature abhors straight lines" is a canon of landscape architecture to the present time.[1] The serpentine curve is a line of visual connection.

Chinoiserie and the English Garden

Either consciously or unconsciously, English landscape designers were influenced by the gardens of China. Although the influence was minor compared with that of classical antiquity and the gardens of Italy, scenes of Chinese life had been filtering into Europe from the sixteenth century, when the sea trade with China began. Europe already knew, or thought that it knew, what a Chinese garden looked like. Daily, Europeans viewed the ubiquitous scenes upon their wallpaper, porcelain, lacquer work, and painted silks and screens. By the middle of the eighteenth century, formal engravings and written accounts of Chinese architecture, gardening, furniture, and costume had reached France and England. Chinoiserie, popular for many years, attained the proportions of a rage. The style-setting aristocracy of France led the way. Ignoring the philosophical and cultural symbolism of Chinese art, as well as simply misunderstanding it, the French turned it into the charming, playful games of childhood that mirrored the delicate and nervous life-style of the salons. There was neither aristocrat nor monarch from the Baltic to the Adriatic who did not possess either a room in the "Chinese taste" or a pagoda in the garden.[2]

The rococo style, by the middle of the eighteenth century, was a frolicsome and very wayward marriage between the classical baroque and the Oriental, stressing naturalistic forms over the idealized abstract forms of the Roman classic. From the beginning of the popularity of Oriental art in Europe in the mid-seventeenth century, its acceptance was marked by a strong ambivalence. Europeans greatly admired its technical excellence and just as strongly detested its content. With its gaudy colors and unfamiliar distortions of perspective and natural forms, Oriental art seemed deformed and naturally grotesque. Either it was received as a perfect source for the expression of "antitaste," particularly in France, or it was so admired for its craftsmanship that Western artisans copied its techniques while altering its content—to the point of depicting round-eyed mandarins perched on monumental Roman ruins, something of a grotesque statement in its own right. Chinoiserie in England, in the mid-eighteenth century, was employed first as an alternative to, and later as an expression of hostility against, the excesses of the worship of the classic and its severe decorum.

Sir William Chambers

The French-inspired rococo style in England had an English look; compared with that of the Continent, the flamboyant decoration was under greater control. Not only did England have a more direct influence from China by way of the British East India Company, but also the influence of France was strongly resisted in England. England also had Sir William Chambers, a respected architect in the Palladian tradition, who as a young man had spent nine years traveling in the Orient in the service of the Swedish East India Company. With the scholarly, apologetic defensiveness of a classical conservative, Chambers published a book of designs in 1757, based on sketches he made in Canton—*Designs of Chinese Buildings, Furniture, Dresses, Machines, and Utensils*. Possibly because of his reputation as a member of the Old Guard and his standing at court (Chambers designed the Royal Gardens at Kew), his work had a widespread influence in England and especially on the Continent.

Chambers explained, very imaginatively, that the Chinese made use of three different kinds of scenes in their artificially constructed gardens: "the pleasing, the horrid, and the enchanted."[3] The pleasing corresponded to the Western idea of the romantic. The horrid was introduced by creating large overhanging rocks, dark caverns, wild cataracts, ill-formed trees that appeared to be twisted and blasted by storms, and "miserable huts," suggesting a state of wretchedness of the inhabitants. The enchanted was created with a play upon contrasts in light and shade, color, and the texture of the plants, as well as the placement of attractive compositions partially hidden by intermediate objects such as shrubs, trees, or rocks. The element of surprise was deliberately introduced to excite the curiosity. Chambers mentioned that the Chinese generally, but not always, avoided straight lines. The zigzagging bridges and winding paths led the eye of the viewer through the garden.

Chambers liked his Chinese designs, but he was aware of the need to defend the frivolity of the taste against the satirical classical horde. "I look upon them as toys in architecture," he wrote, "and as toys are sometimes, on account of their oddity, prettyness, or neatness of workmanship, admitted into the cabinets of the curious, so may Chinese buildings be sometimes allowed a place among compositions of a nobler kind."[4]

The picturesque English garden scene of the 1760s was a composite of the landscapes of Italy (as seen through the paintings of Rosa and Claude) and of Ming porcelain. The carefully designed grounds of the estate consisted most typically of a large, free-form grassy park containing a winding stream and a lake; several small temples in the Gothic, Greco-Roman, and Oriental styles; classical statuary; small architectural ruins; a rocky grotto and a hermit house; and several wooded areas through which serpentine footpaths led the visitor. Arched bridges, frequently of Chinese fretwork design, crossed the streams, and weeping willows drooped their graceful foliage over the edges of the irregular lakes. The pavilions, also called rural retreats, were often concealed behind plantations of trees, some of them imported from America and China.

Unlike the Chinese, who sat on cool slabs of sessel stone or on seats of growing tree roots to contemplate, the English *walked* in their gardens. The English pavilions served as resting places and protection from sudden changes of weather, mood-producing way stations along the path of the stroller from which the sublime views in the park might be observed. They also served as places for picnics, newfangled tea parties, and for small social gatherings.

The pagodas and temples ranged from simple open-air sheds to opulent structures of marble with gilded piers and fretwork. The Oriental buildings were usually made of finished wood that was gaily painted in bright colors. In most cases, they resembled pieces of Meissen porcelain; they were far from what we think of as rustic. The rustic was reserved, as a rule, for open-air seating, for hermitages, and for certain pavilions, and it is these that were destined to survive in the nineteenth century.

The Origin and the Function of the Grotesque in the Gardens

Two structures in the English garden are important to the history of rustic furniture: the grotto and the hermitage. These two buildings were as ubiquitous in the gardens as were grass and trees. Their inappropriateness in England was seldom remarked upon. Dr. Samuel Johnson did observe on one occasion that the damp, cool grotto in the damp, cool climate of England was rather more suitable "for a toad," and Protestant England did have a Roman Catholic past that she greatly preferred to repress, but the grottoes and the hermitages were significantly fashionable objects and we must spend some time considering their meaning.

The history of the ornamental grotto goes back to the most ancient times, and the structure itself can be seen as a primal symbol. Whether human beings emerge from winter hibernation from huts, porticoed villas, or skyscrapers, the springtime renewal of our planet's vegetation has an awesome power to stir our souls. If nothing else, Spring represents visible proof of the earth's well-being, and the budding leaves of plants suggest the possibility of the fertility of the earth. Small wonder that the rites of Spring have been treated in all places and in all times as a celebration. The sacred grove, located near a natural spring or near a waterfall in a rocky mountain gorge, was seen in the ancient world as the place of residence of the Nature deities. Votaries of these gods and goddesses approached the holy spot to express thanksgiving and propitiation in the hope of a bountiful summer harvest. Eventually, in ancient Greece, the sacred grove, in the form of a circular marble temple, was moved to the city and the deities of Nature were attended by selected priests and priestesses.

Natural caves, representing openings into Mother Earth, seem always to have been associated with nature magic and, as a result, have been subjects of a certain ambivalence. A cave offers protection by the great earth mother, but, at the same time, this blissful protection is something of a threat to the independent spirit of man—primitive man could not hide in a cave *and* hunt for food or plant a garden at the same time. In the hot, parched climate of Southern Asia, the natural rocky grotto, containing trickling springs and mosses, came to represent a special gift of the gods. Men did not live in grottoes, but they repaired there for comfort in times of physical or mental stress, much as a child retreats to its own mother under similiar circumstances. Grottoes and stone nymphaeums became the homes of the tutelary deities and the muses—and very sensibly, too, since a grotto was probably the coolest dwelling anywhere in the scorched summers of the ancient world.

Sometime toward the end of the second century B.C., many Eastern religions began to be imported to Italy through the Hellenistic trading centers on the coast of the Tyrrhenian Sea, near the Bay of Naples. This coast is noted for its many natural caves, and, although the coastline has altered through the centuries, ornamented caves have been excavated in this region of Italy. The grotto-caves are believed to have formed a part of landscape gardens attached to summer villas belonging to wealthy Romans of the late Republic and early Empire. The early grottoes in Italy seem to have been associated with the cult of Dionysus (Bacchus) and his uninhibited band of frenzied votaries: satyrs, sileni, fauns, nymphs, and the like. Priapus, another god of fertility, was associated with grottoes, also, as was the goddess Venus.

Decorated grottoes and nymphaeums moved into the new Hellenistic pleasure gardens, either as alcoves hollowed out of stone hillsides or as entire rooms constructed of decorated masonry. Both contained running water and visual representations of the particular deities that they honored. The walls were ornamented with pebble, shell, and colored mosaics, or the masonry was stuccoed with rough pieces of pumice stone (*tufa*), which produced the effect of a natural cave. (This type of grotto work was known as *rustici*.) Some of these garden grottoes have been preserved at Pompeii. Elaborate hydraulic systems were invented to lend theatrical effects to the fountains and miniature waterfalls in grottoes. Even Aristotle had toyed with these inventions. Heron of Alexandria (first century A.D.) designed a fountain containing singing mechanical birds who suddenly grew quiet at the appearance of a mechanical owl.[5] This particular hydraulic tour de force was copied later in the famous owl fountain in the Renaissance garden of the Villa d'Este at Tivoli and the twitterings (or, more likely, "toots") of such *rarae aves* continued to turn up in French and English gardens in the seventeenth and eighteenth centuries. It is difficult to put aside the suspicion that they might once have been used by priests of a religious cult to convince the populace of some mystery.

The manifold arts of the Hellenistic pleasure garden declined along with the politics of Rome in the third century A.D., and it was not until 1300 years later that they were rediscovered.

Late in the fifteenth century, Renaissance searchers after classical remains in Rome excavated the Domus Aurea, the Golden House of Nero (ca. A.D. 65).[6] The Colosseum and the Baths of Titus had been erected on part of the original property. When the excavators reached the underground rooms of the home, they discovered an unfamiliar style of fresco decoration on the walls, one that would have a far-reaching influence upon the future artistic and social life of Europe. The decoration, known collectively as *topia*,[7] consisted of several varieties of deftly painted illusionistic landscape scenes, *trompe l'oeil* architectural details, stucco bas reliefs, and small painted "wallpaper" motifs. The landscape scenes displayed a sophisticated attempt to open up to the outside world the enclosed space of a cool underground room or corridor. In effect, the illusionistic scenes represented an attack upon the wall as a fixed barrier. For the Renaissance, it was a startling discovery. In the early years of the sixteenth century, many additional examples of this decorative style came to light in other regions of Italy. Some of the miniature garden scenes (many of which bear a striking resemblance to Oriental landscape painting) gave a clear picture of a fully developed style of landscape art in which the fusion of Nature and architecture was prominent. One particular painted motif, the arabesque, composed of a series of flowery vertical designs containing highly imaginative animal and plant forms, captured the fancy of Renaissance painters. (Fig. 1-1) Known as "grotesques" to the Renaissance painters, the designs were adapted by such men as Raphael and Guilio Romano to decorate the ceilings and walls of many new villas and palaces. The decoration, fitted into the space in and around paintings of both Christian and pagan subjects, was composed of hybridized monsters, plant forms, and impossible architecture. (Fig. 1-2)

All of this decoration from Roman antiquity, including the rediscovered grottoes, exhibited a freedom, not to say a license, with the powers of the imagination. A few men of the Renaissance found the scenes disturbing. They had also disturbed certain conservative defenders of the austere, puritanical ways of Republican Rome at the time when they were first introduced. The Roman architect Vitruvius wrote in Book VII of *De Architectura* (ca. 30 B.C.):

> Nowadays, all those objects which formerly were copied from reality are scorned by an unreasonable fashion. We now have contemporary fresco paintings of monstrous forms, rather than truthful representations of the familiar world. For example, in the place of columns, they paint fluted reeds with curly leaves and oddly shaped volutes; instead of pediments, they show candelabra supporting arabesque shrines, and on top of the pediments many little flower stalks unroll out of their roots and figures perch atop them, senselessly. Sometimes the stalks support half-length

human figures, sometimes only the heads of both human and animal forms are drawn.

> Such things, however, do not exist; they have never existed, nor shall they ever exist. For how is it possible for a reed to support a roof, or candelabra to lift the weight of a pediment and its ornaments, or that a slender waving stem of a flower can support a figure sitting on it, or that roots and stalks can grow bastardized human figures and flowers, much less both at the same time? . . . The fact is that unreal pictures should not have authoritative approval, even if they are technically excellent. . . .

This passage from Vitruvius has been used as ammunition against artistic irregularity from the time of the late Renaissance to the nineteenth century. John Ruskin, who wrote some very insightful comments on grotesque art, strongly disliked the vulgar extremes to which it descended in Renaissance Venice. Calling the arabesque style a "tissue of nonsense," he wrote:

> If we can draw the human head perfectly, and are masters of its expression and its beauty, we have no business to cut it off, and hang it up by the hair at the end of a garland. If we can draw the human body in the perfection of its grace and movement, we have no business to take away its limbs, and terminate it with a bunch of leaves.[8]

It is difficult for the present age to appreciate Vitruvius' abhorrence of the arabesque designs until we consider that the Romans attached a profound symbolic significance to the plans of architecture, relying upon the orderly sequence of the spatial arrangements to provide psychological control and stability in everyday living.[9] A similar symbolic function was expected of the classical architecture in the Renaissance and also in eighteenth-century England. To the Romans, a sound mind in a sound body meant an orderly mind in an orderly house (and garden). The arabesque designs were illogical, full of curves and disturbing whimsy, and the fusion of the human body with plant forms was an affront to the image of man. Ancient Rome alternately flirted with and castigated Eastern art, much the way the eighteenth century was later to do. The stone grotto—essentially an expensive piece of architecture that amounted to an underground cavern—was the antithesis of Roman regularity. Although it might have been considered an air-conditioned gift of the gods in Greece, the artificially constructed grotto in Italy seemed dark, unnatural, and forbidding. It was unfamiliar to the senses—the very place to set the eager superstitions of the Romans working overtime. (Ghost stories, told at high noon, are rarely successful; they require twilight and shadows and reduced sensory reality for their peculiar power.)

The sixteenth century was captivated by the imaginative possibilities of the garden grottoes. They became the toys, and possibly the working laboratories, of the mannerist artists of that age. We have only to recall the sensation of *déjà vu*, which assails us occasionally when we drive through highway tun-

Fig. 1-1. *Topia* from the House of Livia (Rome, first century B.C.) featuring *trompe l'oeil* column with dragon capital, and winged spirits perched on arabesque candelabra. (Photo: Alinari)

Fig. 1-2. Renaissance grotesques from the ceiling of Villa Bufalini (S. Giustino, Italy), showing imaginative plant, animal, and human forms and impossible architecture. (Photo: Alinari)

nels, to appreciate the boldness of the garden grotto as a form of art. By the end of the sixteenth century, grotto-building was an advanced art. Architects and sculptors sometimes conceived them as fantastic underwater caverns and decorated them accordingly, with sea nymphs, dolphins, marine gods, and exotic fishes. Around the middle of the century, painted walls and tile mosaics gave way entirely to mosaic shell and irregular stone decoration. Bizarrely shaped pieces of *tufa* gave an eerie, netherworld appearance to the alcoves and caves. Grotesque travesties of pastoral scenes, with sculptured sheep and shepherds, were created on the walls, the statuary then being dribbled with lime to make the figures seem part of the walls—living stalactites.[10] Waterworks machines were reinvented to lend both theatricality and prankish humor; to wit: a charming cupid who could whirl around suddenly on his plinth and spit water on the spectator.[11] Much attention was devoted to the *giochi d'acqua*, or water jokes.[12] We know these grottoes from their descendants: carnival fun houses.

Grottoes were also decorated with Christian symbols, particularly the crucifix. The Counter-Reformation in Italy produced some strange hybrids of the sacred and the profane.[13] In the case of the crucifix,

the symbol was used as a quasi-magical fetish. The supernatural religious energy of the crucifix was supposed to annul the demonic power of the grottoes, some of which advertised the nature of their contents by means of hideous, carved stone hell gates. (See photograph on page 12.) The present age will recall that Count Dracula continues to be undone by the appearance of the crucifix and that children still cross their fingers when they wish to undo some lie that they are about to tell. For the most part, however, daring artists (many of whom were closet-heretics) preferred to toy with grotesque demons, nature gods, and secret blasphemy, which they disguised by drawing upon the historically accurate, but flagrantly disreputable classical divinities, Pan, Bacchus, and Priapus.

The Italian grotto was built atop a very narrow psychological abyss, on that tenuous, shifting line between the "funny" as comic and the "funny" as strange or uncanny, which is the natural habitat of the grotesque. The structure was a grimly comic representation of some of the most primitive anxieties in the human mind: those related to man's early struggle to differentiate himself from his surroundings, to exert control over Nature, and to reconcile instinct with civilization, failure to accomplish which, as every child learns early in life, means loss of love, eternal loneliness, and even death. The depiction of the hell gates as devouring mouths shows the archaic nature of the anxiety. If we note the position of the tongue-table inside the "mouth" doorway, illustrated on page 12, we can see the form of many eighteenth- and nineteenth-century hermitages made of roots and twigs. The mouths of the later hermitages, however, will be shaped like Gothic archways.

The hermitage, as a garden adjunct for entertainment, was started at the court of Philip II of Spain, that arch-supporter of the Counter-Reformation. Its arrival in the late sixteenth-century gardens of Italy, however, where the line between pleasure and piety was more distinctly noted than it was in Spain, produced a splitting of the symbolism of the grotto. Well suited to serve in the role of protecting fetish, the hermitage took over that function, freeing the grotto to become wholly demonic.

The hermitage was a small villa, sometimes having an attached alcove for a chapel, and usually it was located near the boundary of the garden. The hermitage in Italy had, in addition, a touch of the magical about it; it was considered good luck to have a hermit resident in one's garden.[14]

In the early development of the Christian Church, a heavy emphasis upon renunciation of the material world, which began as an intrinsic part of reform in contemporary Jewish manners and morals, soon became a fixed attitude. In the Middle Ages, the idea of hermitage developed as an extreme form of total renunciation of the world and, in particular, the flesh. The religious recluse became a symbol of pious mysticism and awesome discipline. Of all the uncomfortable dwellings that hermits chose, the tall column upon which Saint Simeon Stylites spent thirty years was perhaps the most conspicuous. The fact that many religious recluses were psychotic was probably of some significance in the Renaissance because the flirtation with the psychologically bizarre was a strong element in the appeal of the hermitage and the grotto. In this respect, we might recall that a favorite recreation in eighteenth-century London consisted of spending an idle Sunday afternoon visiting the lunatics at Bedlam hospital, the mad laughing at the maddened.

The grotto and the hermitage spread into France around the middle of the sixteenth century. With the French potter Bernard Palissy (ca. 1510–1590), we encounter what might be the first rustic architecture in natural wood, as distinguished from the pumice *rustici* of the earlier Italian grottoes. Palissy was a madman potter who spent years attempting to develop glazes similar to those of Chinese porcelain.[15] He never succeeded in that but he did create *figurines rustiques* and thereby passed on to the seventeenth century a fondness for decorative primeval zoology: lizards, snakes, fish, crustaceans, and also such botanical species as ferns, bramble, ivy, and acorns, all forms prominent in garden mosaics of ancient Italy.

With the knowledge gained from his monomania for the chemistry of glazes and with the help of his favorite Renaissance handbook of allegory, *The Dream of Polifilus*, Palissy turned to grotto work. He published his own book on grotto building in 1563 (*A True Recipe, by which all Frenchmen may learn to add to their treasures*). Palissy built the great grottoes in the Tuileries garden for Catherine de' Medici, complete with suitable moral inscriptions carved over the entrance and his modeled zoological creatures of the dark. He added a touch of underworld splendor to the grottoes by firing the glazed interior decoration, which caused the enamels to fuse into a distorted mass of iridescence. The grottoes no longer exist, but it is known[16] that Palissy wanted to create what he called "grottoes" at the ends of long avenues by using elm trees, "their trunks to serve as columns and their

Fig. 1-3. Shell and stone grotto designed by Isaac de Caus (Woburn Abbey, England, 1626). The shell mosaics exhibit marine gods, nymphs in shell boats, and *putti* riding on dolphins. The grotesque alcove probably contained a fountain at one time. Niches in the walls were designed for statuary. The vaulted grotto opened out onto a garden parterre. (Photo: Reproduced by kind permission of the Marquess of Tavistock and trustees of the Bedford Estates)

leaves and branches arranged as pavilions with windows, frieze, and roof."[17]

The grotto arrived in England early in the seventeenth century, probably with Salomon de Caus, drawing master to the children of James I. A Frenchman from Normandy, de Caus had traveled widely in France and Italy before going to England. He designed several "water projects" for the king and for other English nobles. When Elizabeth, the daughter of James I, married Frederick V of the Palatinate, de Caus was invited to Heidelberg to design the palace gardens and a grotto.[18] De Caus left his son Isaac in England, and it was Isaac who designed the famous garden at Wilton House for the earl of Pembroke in 1615. Isaac de Caus, in the employment of the architect Inigo Jones, also created the grotto at Woburn Abbey in 1626. (Fig. 1-3) John Aubrey, writing in 1691, says:

King Charles Ist did love Wilton above all places: and came thither every Sommer. It was HE, that did put Philip (1st Earle of Pembroke) upon makeing this magnificent Garden and Grotto. . . . Wilton House was the third garden of the Italian mode. But in the time of King Charles II^d, Gardening was much improved and became common: I doe believe, I may modestly affirm, that there is now ten times as much gardening about London as there was in A° 1660; and we have been since that time much improved in foreign plants: especially since about 1683, there have been exotick Plants brought into England, no lesse than seven thousand. [19]

The arrival of the fully developed Italian garden style in England was aborted by the English Civil Wars. The Italian garden had only just made an important dent in a few gardens before Charles I was beheaded and Oliver Cromwell, cutting up many large estates, turned the English pleasure garden into vegetable plots. Upon the return of Charles II from France, gardening flourished according to the classical model of France; however, these earlier Italian gardens have an important bearing upon the garden events in the eighteenth century.

In the seventeenth century, the grotto and the hermitage tended to fuse in meaning at times. We turn again to that most wonderful and indefatigable collector of antiquarian trivia, John Aubrey. Aubrey describes in some detail a grotto designed by Thomas Bushell (1594–1674), page and Seal Bearer to Sir Francis Bacon, and he mentions that Bushell contrived an impromptu entertainment in 1636 for Charles I and his queen with "artificial thunders and lightenings, rain, hail-showers, drums beating, organs playing, birds singing, waters murmuring all sorts of tunes, &c." (Bushell was a talented engineer who taught James I how to drain his tin mines in Cornwall.) Even more interesting is Aubrey's account of Bushell's idea of a hermitage:

> He had donne something (I have now forgott what) that made him obnoxious to the Parliament or Oliver Cromwell, about 1650; would have been hang'd if taken . . . but all that time laye privately in his Howse in Lambeth marsh. . . . In the garret there is a long Gallery, which he hung all with black, and had some death's heads and bones painted. At the end where his Couch was, (was in an old Gothique Nich like an old Monument) painted a Skeleton recumbent on a Matt. At the other end, where was his pallet-bed, was an emaciated dead man stretched out. Here he had several mortifying and divine Motto's. . . . In the time of the Civill Warres his Hermitage over the rocks at Enston were hung with black-bayes [baize]; his bed had black Curtaines, etc., but it had no bed posts but hung by 4 Cordes covered with black-bayes instead of bed-postes. When the Queen-mother came to Oxon to the King, she either brought (as I thinke) or somebody gave her, an entire Mummie from Egypt, a great raritie, which her Majestie gave to Mr. Bushell, but I beleeve long ere this time the dampnesse of the place haz spoyled it with mouldinesse.[20]

Are we to take such satire seriously? Bushell was a charming rakehell, always in debt, always amusing and lovable, who used his inventive genius whilst lying "privately in his Howse in Lambeth marsh," one jump ahead of Cromwell, to make a fashionable caricature of his Puritan pursuers. It is apparent from Aubrey's detailing of the story that he thought it humorous.

At this point, we must pause to examine the function of these garden structures. The grotto is of paramount importance because it appears to be, literally as well as figuratively, the womb of the grotesque (grotto-esque) in Western art. Its ancient association with the world of artistic creativity has been established: the muses dwelled in grottoes. The artist used the emotional sensations and the regressive symbolic thinking evoked by the bizarre caverns for the raw materials of his art. There is, however, a paradox here. The caves are dangerous and damaging to morality; they can be demonic and destructive to the individual and to society, or so it was felt by the conservative party in society. There are a number of hidden elements at work with respect to the decorated grottoes. For one, the grotesque is not the opposite of the beautiful; it is the ridiculous old relative of the sublime and the ideal. Wherever grandiose idealism is displayed, whether in religion, philosophy, or in social systems, the grotesque will always be found lurking somewhere near the edges. It seems to be the role of the grotesque to perceive the discrepancies between the ideal and the real, and it is related to satire, irony, and to visual caricature (all preferred modes of expression in the eighteenth century). Where the grotesque remains at the upper levels of consciousness, it is comic and playfully imaginative, but when it descends to deeper levels, it can, and often does, become sinister and threatening. Neoclassicists are instinctively afraid of it, as we have seen. It is the potentially destructive side of the grotesque that frightens conservative keepers of morality, because in its aggressive, antisocial expression the implied criticism of cultural values can unmask their hollowness, which, in turn, can cause the collapse of a weak system. The grotesque always seems to be outspoken in those eras in which a given set of ideals has already started to decline and strong countermeasures are being taken by the culture to shore up the weaknesses.

Turning to the garden hermitage in England, we find that in most cases during the seventeenth century and the first half of the eighteenth century it was a "horror scene"—a perverse reminder on the edge of a *pleasure* garden of the shortness and the vanity of life. Pensive melancholy, especially of the brooding, religious *memento mori* stripe, sent shivers of masochistic ecstasy through the downtrodden baroque soul of Europe. The hermitage was usually constructed of rough stone or plaster during this time. Around 1750, the architecture shifted to thatched huts made of twigs and roots. The hermitages took on an additional meaning in some of the parks: they became outspokenly and grotesquely comic.

Ernst Kris, in an examination of the comic process, points out an essential element for the comic: What is comic today was terrifying yesterday.[21] This is one of the reasons that some forms of humor become so quickly dated. The comic represents a triumphal mastery over fear. The circus clown burlesquing the sublime feats of the death-defying aerialist whose act preceded him gets his laughs because he is performing on the ground, and also because his gestures malign the bold, graceful aerialist. [22] Here are two representative comments upon the subject of the sublime and the ridiculous from the eighteenth century:

> Whatever is fitted in any sort to excite the ideas of pain and danger, that is to say, whatever is in any sort terrible, or is conversant about terrible objects, or operates in a manner analogous to terror, is a source of the *sublime*. . . . In all these cases, if the pain and terror are so modified as not to be actually noxious; if the pain is not carried to violence, and the terror is not conversant about the present destruction of the person, as these emotions clear the parts, whether fine or gross, of a dangerous and troublesome encumbrance, they are capable of producing delight; not pleasure, but a sort of delightful horror, a sort of tranquillity tinged with terror; which, as it belongs to self-preservation is one of the strongest of all the passions. Its object is the sublime.
> —Edmund Burke, *A Philosophical Enquiry into the Origin of Our Ideas of the Sublime and Beautiful*, 1757.

> [Opposed to the sublime and the pathetic] is the ridiculous: for laughter is an expression of joy and exultation; which arises not from sympathy but triumph; and which seems therefore to have its principle in malignity. Those vices, which are not sufficiently baneful and destructive to excite destestation; and those frailties and errors, which are not sufficiently serious and calamitous to excite pity, are generally such as excite laughter. . . .
> —Richard Payne Knight, *Analytical Inquiry into the Principles of Taste*, 1804.

The eighteenth-century hermitage at mid-century was no longer a sublime horror scene, but a "rural amusement," a disguised, but quite blasphemous triumph over the old Puritan-classical morality of England. (Newspaper advertisements requesting the live-in services of a hermit, or an actor who would pose as one, were not unheard of.) It might be that the secularized garden grotesque has always served to express a sense of outrage against the rigidity of excessive control in whatever tradition it has appeared.

The hermitage, at least, was an *attempt* at triumph. It should be mentioned that there was always a heavy control over Nature in the eighteenth-century garden. After the allegorical stage of development in the parks had been replaced with more expressionistic scenes, the grand landscape views were controlled by means of filtering the composition of natural forms through the technical design organization of landscape painting. Even those who had tired of the sameness of the scenes in the park proper and had fled to the sublime views of "wild nature," in Wales, Scotland, and Switzerland, frequently employed a singular tool for controlling and organizing these overpowering visual experiences—the Claude-mirror. This device was a small convex mirror, sometimes tinted, which helped to "compose" a wild nature scene. The user stood with his back to the scene and viewed the ruined abbeys, mountains, cataracts, or turbulent skies and seas through the mirror. The nature poet Thomas Gray considered the Claude-mirror a wonder of its time.

Until mid-century, the hermitage and the grotto were present in the gardens more or less as separate entities. Queen Caroline put Merlin, the magician-wizard, into a Gothic niche in her grotto at Richmond in 1735. [23] The wax Merlin and his ilk elicited howls of derision from the satirists. The grotto and the hermitage began to condense into the single hermitage around 1750, near the time that the Chinese pagodas entered the parks. The hermitage remained a pivotal symbol in the gardens, slippery as a serpentine eel, as the grotesque is ever.

The Eighteenth-Century Furniture

Rustic furniture is a grotesque joke, at times even a joke within a joke. The concept of a rustic chair is unusually sophisticated, not primitive, as it would appear at first sight. For its strangely mirthless success, it requires a built-in ambiguity in the visual interplay between the naturalistic materials from which it is fashioned and the unmistakable evidence of the wit of its human builder. The balance between the two must be arranged in such a way to allow for *sudden* shifts of attention—from Man to Nature, and back again to Man. Commonly, furniture is made up of structural and ornamental features that have been abstracted and condensed from Nature. For example, it is implicitly understood that the form of a spiral post has been borrowed from Nature's pattern of a spiral vine; for a chairmaker to use a wooden post that has, in reality, been grooved by a natural vine causes the form to become explicit. The surprise inherent in the sudden illumination of form is something of a joke all by itself, but if the craftsman takes these real forms one step farther and mixes them with an artistically refined design, then he has created a caricature, a subtle mockery of stylish furniture (and one that both Rusticus and fashion-weary Urbanus can be amused by).

In the chair in figure 1-4 this ambiguity is stunningly successful. Materials that appear naturalistic have been used to make a chair whose lines are associated with "genteel" elegance. The eye shifts back and forth between the formal design and the exaggerated grotesqueness of the rustic material; moreover, the material is used without idealized abstraction from Nature (except for sawing off the ends of the branches, that is). For a contemporary analogy to this eighteenth-century chair, imagine the well-known Mies van der Rohe Barcelona chair, its handsome tufted leather seat and back supported not by the lyrical lines

Fig. 1-4. Rustic chair, ca. 1770. (Photo: Courtesy of the Victoria
and Albert Museum, London)

of gleaming steel, but rather with natural hickory or white oak poles, the rough bark still intact.

Art is a special variety of communication; there is a sender, there is a receiver, and there is a message. Contrary to our usual way of speaking, an artist does not create, he re-creates; that is, the artist takes in visual-tactile sense perceptions, mixes them with his own emotions and ideas, and then invents a new way of expressing what his senses have recorded. Usually, the artist destroys, or reduces in some way, part of his material in the process of reshaping it to express an ideal conception;[24] the sculptor chisels away part of the stone, the furniture maker cuts away part of the wood. The great novelty of rustic furniture is that this destruction does not occur, or it is, at least, very minimal.

A chair, of all objects of furniture, is probably the most heavily invested with body symbolism. Our first chairs were our parents' laps. The mother-chair is curvaceous and soft; the father-chair is harder, more angular, and larger. A chair partially encloses the body and has contact with the parts of the body whose names we then transfer to the parts of the chair. (In the late Victorian era, a chair leg was called a chair *limb*.) It is this early tactile experience of sitting in parental laps that accounts for the chair's becoming a symbol of authority: a throne represents a king, the *cathedra* represents a bishop, and the leader of a meeting is said to "have the chair."

It is for these reasons that the function and the form and decoration of chairs can tell us more about the social customs and attitudes of Western people than can any other object of furniture. For example, the builder of the root chairs shown in figure 1–5 has shaped two seats merely by bending a resistant material. What is the message in this? Viewing the chair in its eighteenth-century context, I suspect that the artist is saying that he is tired of being cut and shaped

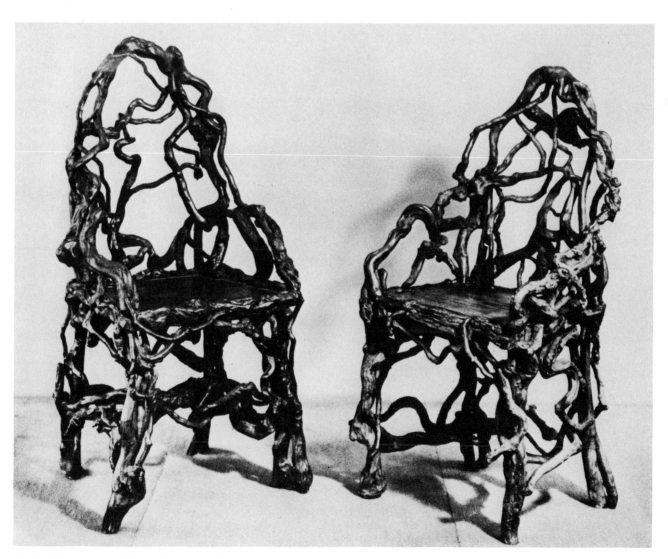

Fig. 1-5. Root chairs, eighteenth century. (Photo: Courtesy of David Tremayne, Ltd., London)

along the lines of the classical model. He is also saying that he wants the parts of his body, warts and all, to be joined together as Nature intended. He does not wish to have the tops of his legs separated from his seat by guardian Roman lion heads, nor by mathematically proportioned architectural motifs; he does not want his back to be held ramrod straight in imitation of ceremonial dignity. The chair parts are to flow freely and with intricate natural connection. Static symmetry is to be left to the unnatural despots; the natural man does not need it. The artist makes his aggressive joke by giving his chairs to a hermit—the ultimate symbol of denial of bodily freedom of sensation. The pot is calling the kettle black, but in this case the artist has besooted them both, creating a joke within a joke.

It is unfortunate that the surviving furniture for eighteenth-century summerhouses is rare. There are, however, a number of stylebooks and tradesmen's cards of the period available for examination. Among the stylebooks most influential to the Chinese-Gothic taste were:

William and John Halfpenny, *New Designs for Chinese Temples, Triumphal Arches, Garden Seats, Palings, &c.* (1750–1752)

Edwards and Darly, *A New Book of Chinese Designs* (1754)

Charles Over, *Ornamental Architecture in the Gothic, Chinese, and Modern Taste . . .* (Many of which may be executed with roots of trees) for gardens, parks, forests, woods, canals, &c. containing palings of several sorts, gates, garden-seats both close and open, umbrellos, alcoves, grottoes, and grotesque seats, hermitages, triumphal arches, temples, banqueting houses and rooms, rotundos, observatories, icehouses, bridges, boats, and cascades . . . (1758)

Thomas Chippendale, *The Gentleman and Cabinet-Maker's Director*, 3d edition (1762)

Robert Manwaring, *The Cabinet and Chair-maker's Real Friend and Companion* (1765)

William Wrighte, *Grotesque Architecture, or Rural Amusement* (1767)

On July 13, 1754, there appeared an advertisement in Jackson's *Oxford Journal* for "Garden Seats, Windsor and Forrest Chairs and Stools, in the modern Gothic, and Chinese Taste . . ." from one William Partridge, cabinetmaker.[25] The date of this advertisement is noteworthy. Before the middle of the century, there does not appear to be evidence in any European country of the existence of seats that looked as if they had been constructed, with studied rustic intent, from logs and branches of trees. The Venetian sculptor and furniture maker, Andrea Brustolon (1662–1723), is perhaps an exception. A pupil of the Baroque sculptor Filippo Parodi, who was a member of the school of Bernini, Brustolon is remarkable not only as a sculptor, but also as a practitioner of the grotesque. He has left behind a number of carved chairs and several groups of sculpture in wood, now preserved in the Ca' Rezzónico in Venice, which were designed as masterful, but quite bizarre pedestals to support Chinese porcelain vases.[26] One of his chairs is a piece of sculpture made up of visual puns. The arms are carved natural tree limbs, a pun on *braccio*, the Italian word for *arm* as well as for *branch*. The feet are carved boots, or, to be more exact, they are boots in the process of metamorphosis from natural wood. The ends of the toes have been carved to resemble the sawn ends of tree limbs; the heels of the boots are still spurs of a natural tree, while the upper parts of the boots have already been transformed into leather. Spiral vines, or foliage, climb upward over the boots. In the Museo Civico in Belluno, Brustolon's birthplace, there is a sketch for a chair with similar lines. (Fig. 1-6) Brustolon's sketch shows crossed rungs and spiraling vines around the chair's limbs. The grotesque faces on the drawing might have been intended as sculptural ornaments for the chair, or perhaps for the upholstery—Brustolon also designed the needlepoint tapestry for his chairs.

Fig. 1-6. Sketch for a chair by Andrea Brustolon (1662–1723). (Photo: Courtesy of the Museo Civico, Belluno, Italy)

In England, the traditional "rural" seats of the country people, cut off from the fashionable towns by impassable roads, were wooden benches, stools, settles, ladder-back "chayres," stick-back Windsor chairs, and the ancient basketwork chairs constructed of willow or coiled straw. The country chairmaker worked exclusively in these traditional styles until the stylebooks of the mid-eighteenth century arrived—simultaneously with improved roads and highways.[27] Both Windsor and wickerwork chairs traditionally were used out of doors in English summers, but not, it seems, in the most fashionable Anglo-Chinese gardens of midcentury aristocrats. Mr. Partridge's advertisement suggests that he was primarily a maker of Windsor chairs now producing a lively product, garden seats in the "modern taste." We wonder where he obtained his patterns and when.

There were at least three types of rustic chairs in England between 1750 and 1770. The earliest was probably the root furniture used in the similarly constructed hermitages. (See fig. 1-5.) A second type was the practical rustic settee, called a forest chair, which was in all probability used along serpentine paths in wooded areas (as they were at the Virginia Springs). Figure 1-7 shows a trade card dating from the late eighteenth century. John Gloag mentions in *The Englishman's Chair* that the drawings on this trade card were taken from printers' stock cuts dating from several decades earlier. Neither the forest chair shown in the lower right of the trade card nor the hermit's chairs in figure 1-5 bear any resemblance to the kind of post-and-lintel rustic work or the woven wattle that is as old as primitive man in the British Isles, and which was so well described by Daniel Defoe in *Robinson Crusoe* (1719). The third category is the genre to which the chair in figure 1-4 belongs. Apparently developing in the 1760s, chairs of this type are satirical fashion-pieces, which could have been used in a more elegant "Chinese" pavilion or in a rural banqueting house. This chair takes us directly to the Chinese problem.

The storm of controversy over Chinoiserie reached a peak between 1750 and 1760. Chinoiserie was basically a matter of interior decoration, and even as such it was confined to ladies' bedchambers and to lesser rooms. Classical ideals, officially, still held sway

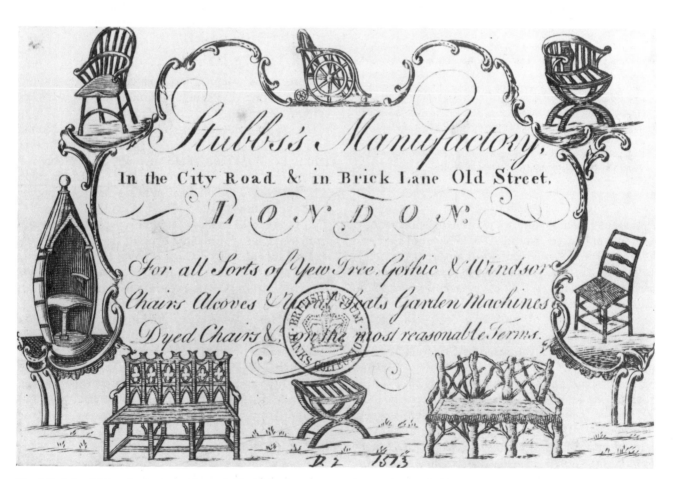

Fig. 1-7. Late eighteenth-century trade card. Clockwise from top left: Windsor chair; "garden machine," used for wheeling the elderly and the infirm through large gardens; Windsor captain's chair with a curule base; rush-bottomed ladder-back chair; "forest chair"; curule stool; Gothic settee; coiled straw "alcove chair." (Photo: Courtesy of the Trustees of the British Museum)

27

in the Palladian architecture of the houses, in the formal rooms of the house and in the garden. The Chinese pagoda, however, had begun to spread into the gardens. Depending upon one's point of view, garden Chinoiserie was idealistic or it was a gaudy, grotesque protest against the classic. We have to recall that the Italian landscape scenes in the older parks were composed of marble statues, stone buildings, ruins, broad expanses of green grass and trees, sky tones, and essentially cool, somber colors. The early eighteenth century took its melancholy quite seriously. Apart from flowering shrubs, parterres near the houses, and a few borders of flowers, the parks and gardens were without bright color during most of the year. The painted pagodas must have seemed startlingly garish and lively by contrast. Chinoiserie took up the rebellious role that had been played by the grotto in imperial Rome and in the late Renaissance. The Chinese Taste had to battle against the existing classical establishment, and the arguments against it—there were hundreds—have a familiar ring:

> . . . what shall we say of the taste and judgment of those who spend their lives and their fortunes in collecting pieces, where neither perspective, nor proportion, nor conformity to nature are observed; I mean the extravagant lovers and purchasers of CHINA, and INDIAN screens. I saw a sensible foreigner astonished at a late auction, with the exorbitant prices given for these SPLENDID DEFORMITIES, as he called them, while an exquisite painting of Guido passed unnoticed, and was set aside as unfashionable lumber. Happy should I think myself to be able to convince the fair connoisseurs that make the greatest part of Mr. Langford's audiences, that no genuine beauty is to be found in whimsical and grotesque figures, the monstrous offspring of wild imagination, undirected by nature and truth.
> —*The World* (28 June 1753).

So far as it can be determined, the use of tree roots suddenly appeared around 1750. Who would expend the energy and hard labor to uncover tree roots to make a basketwork stool or to use for architectural purposes? Possibly a Chinese peasant who had no other wood to use or, in England, a country of forests—albeit rapidly diminishing ones—an English decorator in search of expressive novelty.

Rustic latticework was used in China as building material, much as was bamboo. The lattice was lashed together at the points of intersection with a simple cross-tie and knot (or, in the case of some rustic roots and twigs, fastened together with wooden dowels). Traditionally, the ropes were made of natural materials: coconut fibers in Japan,[28] silk ropes in China.[29] Observe the carved cross-ties, resembling silk cords, binding the seat rails and the branches of the back of the chair in figure 1-4.

The depth of feeling for trees among the Chinese and the people of India was akin to their regard for mountains, water, and rocks. Early European visitors to China marveled at the horticultural skills that produced the deliberately twisted, dwarfed, and stunted trees in Chinese gardens. The art of dwarfing and miniaturizing trees was then a highly esteemed, secret craft, and the production of such trees was the main task of Chinese gardeners.[30] Anyone who has worked with the espaliering of fruit trees will realize how simple it is to produce a "living seat" from the carefully pruned and bent limbs of trees. All that is required is time, a length of time that would have been commercially prohibitive for a businessman-cabinetmaker trying to supply a booming market. It is this time factor that accounts for the *carving* of rustic furniture.

Let us move forward to Robert Manwaring's stylebook of 1765. Manwaring includes fourteen garden seats, five of which are in the style of the seats shown in figures 1-8 and 1-9. Manwaring avers:

> These are the only Designs of the Kind that ever were published. . . . I hope they will give general Satisfaction with respect to their Grandeur, Variety, Novelty and Usefulness; and if I succeed in this Point, I shall think myself amply satisfied for the Time and Trouble I have been at in composing them.

"Time and Trouble"? This is a strange interjection into his preface. Perhaps Manwaring anticipated some dispute about how much originality his rural chairs contained.

The chair in figure 1-4 is one of a set of six chairs, dated ca. 1770, now in the Victoria and Albert Museum, London. The chairs actually are carved of beechwood, covered with gesso, and painted brown. Whether they were made after Manwaring's designs, we do not know.

In figure 1-10 is shown a Chinese painting on silk from the Ch'ing dynasty. Among the several items of furniture displayed in the picture are two rustic stools constructed from the boles and roots of four inverted saplings. The roots have been interwoven to form a strong apron to support the square, drop-in seat. Notice the configuration and the taper of the legs on the musician's stool in the detail. (Fig. 1-11) When the legs of this stool are compared with those of the chair in figure 1-4 and with Manwaring's designs, the source of Manwaring's chairs (he used the slightly old-fashioned term, back-stool) becomes evident. The arrangement of the knotholes on the Chinese stool and also on Manwaring's seats suggests that of fruitwood.

It is my strong feeling that the design source of Manwaring's chairs was originally a Chinese stool, that an enterprising sea captain saw such primitive stools in Canton and brought some of them home to

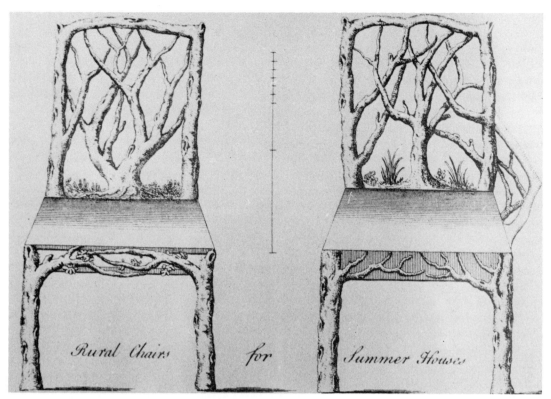

Fig. 1-8. Designs for rustic chairs from Robert Manwaring, *The Cabinet and Chair-maker's Real Friend and Companion* (1765).

Fig. 1-9. Rustic settee by Robert Manwaring. The classical busts, used as finials on the back posts, have slightly moronic expressions.

England, where their potential for novelty was quickly exploited by craftsmen and decorators.

This tentative theory of the Chinese origins of root furniture rests upon the future investigation of the folk crafts of China, and possibly India. For lack of research materials, I cannot verify it at the moment. It is always possible that the Western hermitage and the hermitage furniture made of twigs and roots developed from indigenous grotesque sources—perhaps the winter appearance of tangled, dead-looking vines covering pergolas and entrances to grottoes. Certainly, grotesque tree roots and limbs with the rough bark intact served as England's substitute for the rustic *tufa* of Italy. Still, the coincidence of the Chinese influence upon the rococo in Europe raises a question about rustic materials. I do not believe that the rococo distortion of the content of Oriental art at the hands of Western designers was so naive as we have been in the habit of thinking. Designers made use of Chinese art as artists, not as anthropologists. It is interesting to observe the ambivalent attitude of the West toward Oriental forms of art in the seventeenth and eighteenth centuries; as usual, what began as a protest, ended by being assimilated. We are still sitting in Chinese Chippendale chairs. They might, in fact, be more Chinese than we have heretofore realized.

Fig. 1-11. Detail of fig. 1-10.

Fig. 1-10. Chinese painting on silk, *The Sound of Music*, Ch'ing dynasty.

30

The painted *prunus* blossoms on Manwaring's rural chairs were once carved in pierced-cut aprons upon Chinese and Indian rosewood furniture. It is also possible that some Chinese furniture with carved aprons of stylized branch forms descended from folk stools of the type shown in figure 1-10, much as Chippendale's elegant ladder-back chairs, with their abstract, interwreathed "ladders," had their genesis in fourteenth-century English ladder-back chairs with, perhaps, an assist from rustic furniture.

Turning to another eighteenth-century designer, we encounter a gentle wit whose rococo imagination had a great influence upon Chinoiserie decoration in England—Matthew Darly (also called Mathias Darly). From 1750 to 1754, Darly issued a series of engraved designs for Chinese decoration which encompass everything from Chinese philosophers to dragon boats. Figures 1-12 and 1-13 show three chairs designed by Darly for his stylebook of 1754. All of the several chair designs in that book, as well as pedestals for displaying porcelain vases and a few writing tables, show these grotesque legs, rooted to the ground.

Figs. 1-12 and 1-13. Designs for root chairs by Mathias Darly, from Edwards and Darly, *A New Book of Chinese Designs (1754)*. Darly's furniture exhibits the strongest possible effort to show itself all of a piece. (Photos: Reproduced from the Rare Book Collection of the Library of Congress, Washington, DC)

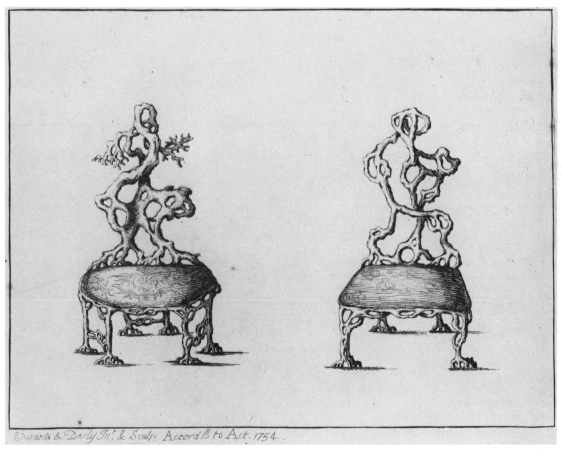

Edwards & Darly Invt. & Sculp. Accordg. to Act. 1754.

Darly's whimsical drawings of roots are unlike those of any other designer. It would be interesting to know whether Darly intended the feet on his furniture as a conventional representation of roots or whether he wanted the roots literally planted in the ground. Note that the base of the chair at left in figure 1-12 resembles the burgomeister's chair, an adaptation of an Asian chair that appeared in Holland in the seventeenth century. The balloon-back chair in figure 1-13 we shall encounter again in the nineteenth century.

The most famous stylebook of the eighteenth century was and is Thomas Chippendale's *The Gentleman and Cabinet-Maker's Director*, known simply as the *Director*. It was first published in 1754, with a second edition coming out the following year. A third, enlarged edition was issued in installments between 1759 and 1762.

The *Director* shows a wide variety of popular furniture styles in the rococo, Chinese, and Gothic tastes, then being made by many other London cabinetmakers as well as by Chippendale. The drawings of the furniture in the rococo style are full of S and C curves, which served to soften or to obscure the functional construction features in the furniture. The curved shapes were antithetical to classical styles of furniture, which tend to emphasize the separateness of each part of the construction. It is fairly clear that some of the drawings were intended as design ideas, rather than for exact copying, but literal-minded cabinetmakers in the authoritarian atmosphere of classical England objected that many of the designs were structurally unsound. Chippendale was then put into the position of defending the designs, and he insisted repeatedly that they could indeed be realized. The controversy over who designed Chippendale has raged over the years.

Rustic furniture does not appear in the *Director* until the third edition, and, significantly, the single plate was engraved by Matthew Darly. (Fig. 1-14) Darly's experiments with the imaginative world of the grotesque are evident in many of his plates for the *Director*, especially in his treatment of birds and animals. (Rarely does he distort a human face or figure.) Goats and owls are metamorphosed into gargoyles (uniting

Fig. 1-14. Garden seats engraved by Darly for Thomas Chippendale, *The Gentleman and Cabinet-Maker's Director*, 3d ed. (1761). Left to right: French chair with alternate rustic leg; French settee; grotto chair.

the classical with the Gothic); dolphins and birds have the ambiguous forms of dragons and reptiles (uniting the classical with the Chinese).

Of the three designs for garden seats that appeared in the *Director*, two are chairs and one is a long French-style settee, which "may be placed in Walks, or at the Ends of Avenues." The chair on the left is a carved French chair with a trophy of garden tools for the back. The only hint of the rustic is contained in the alternate design for the front leg, on the left. It is a small sapling—very small. One suspects that Chippendale was not disposed to creating travesties of his own furniture. He states that the chair is suitable "for Arbours, or Summer-Houses." The chair on the right is a grotto chair. The carved, open scallop shell would have been silver gilt or painted to look like mother-of-pearl, and the legs would have been silver- or gold-leafed. The legs of this chair resemble Chinese goldfish, instead of the usual dolphins; the drooping fins at the mouth are reminiscent of a mandarin's moustache, another of Darly's little jokes. (See also fig. 1-15 for another example of grotto furniture.)

The *Director* contains also nine designs of chairs "after the Chinese manner . . . very proper for a Lady's Dressing Room: especially if it is hung with India paper." Chippendale adds that "they will likewise suit Chinese Temples. They have commonly Cane-Bottoms, with loose cushions; but, if required, may have stuffed Seats, and Brass Nails." These chairs are the square-legged, rectilinear Chinese Chippendale chairs, with their fretwork panels, that we are accustomed to seeing in mahogany. In the early years of the twentieth century, these chairs were copied in rustic wood.

The Chinese chairs are a subtle blend of static control and movement. The diagonal lines in the fretwork panels set up a sense of outward movement from a central point; the framework in which they are placed, however, keeps this movement within bounds. The squared space at the intersections of the legs and the seat is softened by the addition of curved brackets. Similarly, the rake of the seat back and the angled back legs tend to offset the squareness of the basic form of the chair. It seems to be vouchsafed to certain designs throughout the centuries to express an optimum blend of contrasting tendencies. The Chinese Chippendale chairs fit this category.

Rustic furniture served its function of protest in the eighteenth century and then transferred its duty to the middle-class *cottage ornée* in the late part of the century. As we shall see in the next chapter, rustic work was absorbed into the decorative features of these middle-class vacation retreats. They were, of course, hermitages.

Fig. 1-15. Grotto table. Probably a late nineteenth- or early twentieth-century reproduction from southern Europe. The central post, tripod legs, and supports for the top are style features of Gothic period tables seen in medieval manuscripts. (Photo: Courtesy of the Kunstgewerbemuseum, Staatliche Museen Preussicher Kulturbesitz, West Berlin)

CHAPTER 2

The Nineteenth and Early Twentieth Centuries

England

The familiar "tapestry of history" metaphor—in which a given historical age is seen as made up of many woven strands of yarn, each spun from many parallel fibers, which have been dyed in many colors—becomes in the intricate warp and weft of the early nineteenth century a document of the very processes of history itself: The strands that make up the tapestry of that era were spun on the spinning jenny and woven on the power loom in the factories of the Industrial Revolution. Increasingly, from the last years of the reign of George III onward, the new machines required that men, women, and children who had lived quietly for centuries in villages and on small farms give up the land and their individual cottage crafts and industries and move into factories in rapidly swelling cities. The overcrowded, crime-ridden, wretched social conditions of that day have been well documented.

One strand from the tapestry can be traced to the developing passion of Englishmen for picturesque natural scenery, which first began to be evident around 1750, when a certain boredom with the landscape garden crept in. William Shenstone, who seems always to have been in the vanguard of eighteenth-century taste and whose garden at the Leasowes was an early showplace to which 150 people might pilgrimage each Sunday, wrote in an "Elegy" (ca. 1748):

> On the world's stage I wish'd some sprightly part;
>   To deck my native fleece with tawdry lace;
> 'Twas life, 'twas taste, and—oh my foolish heart!
>   Substantial joy was fix'd in pow'r and place.
>
> . . . .

> Oft too I pray'd, 'twas nature form'd the pray'r,
>   To grace my native scenes, my rural home;
> To see my trees express their planter's care,
>   And gay, on Attic models, raise my dome.
>
> But now 'tis o'er, the dear delusion's o'er!
>   A stagnant breezeless air becalms my soul:
> A fond aspiring candidate no more,
>   I scorn the palm, before I reach the goal. [1]

Shenstone traded the scenes of the Leasowes for the romantic view of the simple life at an "Inn at Henley" (1751):

> To thee, fair freedom! I retire
>   From flattery, cards, and dice, and din:
> Nor art thou found in mansions higher
>   Than the low cott, or humble inn.
>
> . . . .
>
> I fly from pomp, I fly from plate!
>   I fly from falsehood's specious grin!
> Freedom I love, and form I hate,
>   And chuse my lodgings at an inn. [2]

A new word was coined to describe the passionate searcher after the wild scenery of the British Isles: *tourist*.[3] The tourists systematically explored the northern Lake District, the mountains of Scotland and Wales, and the enchanted ruins and landscapes of Ireland. Their enthusiastic published accounts of their tours created a great vogue for travel on foot in the wilder outlying regions of Britain. The volume of summer tourism increased enormously. In 1807, Robert Southey described the scene perfectly:

Within the last thirty years a taste for the picturesque has sprung up;—and a course of summer travelling is now looked upon to be as essential as ever a course of spring physic was in old times. While one of the flocks of fashion migrates to the sea-coast, another flies off to the mountains of Wales, to the lakes in the northern provinces, or to Scotland; some to mineralize, some to botanize, some to take views of the country,—all to study the picturesque, a new science for which the English have discovered a new sense in themselves, which assuredly was not possessed by their fathers. . . .[4]

An important effect of this travel on foot was the urban gentleman's rediscovery of the native, ancient architecture of Britain. The tours induced an increasing awareness of, and interest in, England's medieval history. The Gothic Taste had emerged in the 1740s, slightly before the great Chinoiserie rage, when both styles were expressions of resistance to the classic, but the rococo-Gothic detached itself from Chinoiserie and continued on beneath the surface of the late eighteenth- and early nineteenth-century neoclassical styles. In the 1820s and 1830s, the Gothic rose to prominence. The romantic era had arrived. The hue and cry of critics eager to replace the meaningless, repetitive classical styles of the eighteenth century with something more expressive was heard—and read—up and down the land. The problem was that there was ambivalence and uncertainty in the development of a fresh style.

The Gothic Revival

No single style emerged as dominant; nonetheless, England held, in general, an abiding affection for natural, picturesque settings and some form of style and decoration from her own past. Any kind of building up to the time of Sir Christopher Wren was acceptable as the locus for Merry Olde England: Plantagenet castles, Gothic abbeys, and Tudor dwellings of timber, or Jacobean gatehouses. Serious scholarship in medieval history was just in the beginning stages. Sir Walter Scott was an important influence on the taste for medieval matters. His novels were ransacked for stimulating ideas and for useful precepts of high chivalric morality. Rusty, creaking suits of armor were polished up and *worn* in re-creations of jousting tournaments.

Even before Horace Walpole's Gothic pastiche at Strawberry Hill in the middle of the eighteenth century, searchers after the Gothic had been raiding cathedral towns for discarded stained glass windows and bobbin-turned chairs. The rustic twigwork hermitage in estate parks had become associated with the Gothic Taste early on.

The Gothic style of the twelfth through the fifteenth centuries was a Northern European "barbarian" architecture that had its oldest roots in Celtic art. Totally different from the calm, controlled simplicity of the Hellenic, Celtic art was a painfully intricate, continuous, actively moving, asymmetrical congregation of pure lines. (This was true also of the art of other Northern races.) The complexity in the organization of Celtic drawing and decoration makes it impossible to assimilate at a glance; a series of separate visual encounters is required before it can be taken in.[5]

Five hundred years later, like a Northern phoenix, this complex multiplicity was revived in the stones, grotesque sculpture, and stained glass of the Gothic cathedrals. The form was slim and linear. The parts were multiple and without boundaries. The lines flew off the silhouettes of spiked points and spires into the empyrean. Celtic magic, profundity of Northern feeling, and enthusiastic religious union with mystical Nature—all of these stunning emotions are evoked by the visual experience of the cathedrals. The effect is a continuous line running from the finite and soaring into the infinite, and this was the intent. The Celt has never succeeded, or wanted to succeed, in making sharp visual distinctions between the rational and the irrational, considering both to be a part of himself; this is an attitude deeply imbedded in Celtic folklore and in Celtic art. It is also sharply opposed to the Hellenic need for boundaries and its "fear of the indefinite."[6]

When, in the early nineteenth century, the reality of an inadequately balanced life in the cities became intolerable and a new technology had outstripped the capacity of governmental institutions to deal with it, England looked back with sympathetic understanding to her own past and found, if not insight, at least an old method of coping with material agony: One escaped to fantasy and to immaterial sensation. The impoverished used gin; the well-to-do headed for other times, other places. The architect of the nineteenth century became a designer of stage sets. No less an influential critic than John Ruskin declared, "We want no new style of architecture. . . . The forms of architecture already known are good enough for us. . . ."[7]

At the beginning of a renewed interest in the Gothic, we (along with the artist) can see the incongruous and inharmonious marriage of Northern art with the Southern classical in Charles Over's design for a rustic hermitage, published in 1758. (Fig. 2-1) Over's hermit dwells in a horizontal Palladian villa with a central hall and two symmetrical wings. The dynamic lines and the points of the interlaced tree roots, however, are anything but reposed. They are like so many flames, or earthworms, barely held down by the controlled symmetry of the framework and the roof. Soon (fig. 2-2), they will grow into slender Celtic reptiles with long tails and fancy topknots and they will raise the roof to reach toward "up," which is the expression of the native spirit of the Celt's freedom of imagination and lack of concern with the limits of reality and earthbound rules (except where they affect his personal freedom). If the celebration of Man was the business of the Greeks, states of the spirit were matters of vital interest to the Northern races.

Nineteenth-century England contained a severe split in its spirit. On the one hand, there was an old, established, landed ruling class that had been educated exclusively and for many generations in the tradition of the classical Renaissance. On the other, this tradition was breaking down at precisely the time that a new, more aggressive group of people, drawn from the folk and the "Celtic fringe" of Britain's old villages, were gaining strength and political power. Once the middle class achieved a certain level of power, classically educated taste was crowded from its position of dominance and supplanted with a love of sensation and gleeful, ebullient ostentation—both deep-rooted characteristics of ancient Celtic culture.

With moving eloquence, John Ruskin expressed the *Zeitgeist* of his own day in a lecture on architecture to a group of influential Edinburgh citizens in 1853:

> Walk round your Edinburg buildings, and look at the height of your eye, what you will get from them. Nothing but square-cut stone—square-cut stone—a wilderness of square-cut stone for ever and for ever; so that your houses look like prisons, and truly are so; for the worst feature of Greek architecture is, indeed, not its costliness, but its tyranny. These square stones are not prisons of the body, but graves of the soul; for the very men who could do sculpture like this . . . are here! still here, in your despised workmen: the race has not degenerated, it is you who have bound them down, and buried them beneath your Greek stones. There would be a resurrection of them, as of renewed souls, if you would only lift the weight of these weary walls from off their hearts.[8]

The Vine-covered Cottage

Because manufacturers and tradesmen no longer needed to live above their business establishments and their increasing wealth enabled them to build retreats well out of the dismal industrial towns, commercial architects, beginning in the early 1820s, conducted a thriving business in designing and publishing plans for middle-class country cottages, villas, and manor houses.

Fig. 2-1. Design for a hermitage by Charles Over, *Ornamental Architecture in the Gothic, Chinese, and Modern Taste. . . .* (1758). The distortion of the crucifix finial on the hermitage is characteristic throughout the eighteenth and nineteenth centuries. (Photo: Reproduced from the Special Collection of the Library of the University of Virginia)

Fig. 2-2. Garden banqueting room from Charles Over (1758).

36

Now was invented the vine-covered cottage. The *cottage ornée*, as it was termed, was a charming, picturesque dwelling "embosomed in trees and shrubs," as if it had grown there. The landscape site was equally important as the architecture of the cottage. The house (called a country-box by acid-tongued satirists in the eighteenth century who resented the tradesman's pretensions to gentility and the unheard-of leisure to take a weekend off from his shop in the city) was decorated with Gothic, or other "Olden Time," decorative features and rustic work. Both the porches, constructed of rustic trees and branches, and the small summerhouses were meant to be covered with vines. It was this picturesque country-box that had such a far-reaching influence upon nineteenth-century American domestic architecture, and, as in England, it was the same earnest longing to escape from the depressing, crowded cities to Nature, to simplicity, upright morality, and space that created it.

In figure 2-3 is pictured an ornamented cottage from Richard Brown's *Domestic Architecture* (1842). Brown's accompanying remarks are of interest.

. . . the house will require to be composed of irregular and diversified parts; the summits of the masses to be various, of unequal height, and playful and angular forms of different magnitudes and projections; some of which parts are to be seen entire, whilst others are partially hid by overhanging branches of trees, or enwrapped in ivy climbing over the roof, and up the chimney shafts, or otherwise hanging in festoons. . . . The awning [porch] is designed for a shady piazza, or shelter against the summer heat; here the occupant may take his exercise, read, and meditate quietly, or with his family sit on rustic seats and enjoy the beauties of nature which surround their dwelling. Such an appropriate appendage as the awning to the rustic cottage is most properly formed of trunks of unbarked trees, surmounted with a tasteful Chinese Cornice above, (from which those objects had their origin,). . . . The trunks or rough columns should have Virginia creepers with sweet Clematis, and China roses planted near them, to which they will climb and grow up: thus forming a most delightful, fragrant, and rural bower.[9]

Fig. 2-3. A *cottage ornée*. Richard Brown, *Domestic Architecture* (1842). Note the rustic settee at rear right.

Richard Brown's book was one of many such style-books. The most comprehensive work in this genre was J.C. Loudon's *Encyclopedia of Cottage, Farm and Villa Architecture* (1832); as early as 1804, however, Edmund Bartell, Jun., had published *Hints for Picturesque Improvements in Ornamented Cottages*. Rustic work had declined in the neoclassical atmosphere of the very end of the eighteenth century. Bartell writes of the "forest seat" as if it were a revival of the style: "I have seen chairs made of the twisted branches of the oak or elm, truly grotesque, and well adapted to the cottage garden."[10]

One final comment from the London architects will help to place rustic work in its proper setting. The Swiss chalet became a popular style of cottage architecture in the 1840s, and it was usually featured among the several types of domestic houses in the pattern books. In *How to Lay Out a Garden or Landscape Gardening* (1852), Edward Kemp wrote:

> A rustic arbour will not . . . be an unfit accompaniment to a building in the Swiss character, or even to some kinds of house Gothic . . . but it would be entirely inharmonious with a building in the Greecian [*sic*] or Italian manner, which demands more artistic and classical attendants.[11]

The picturesque, rustic *cottage ornée* sets the scene for the arrival of rustic work in America in the early nineteenth century.

America

Very little of the English landscape movement reached America in the eighteenth century. The picturesque plantation estates of the South, for example, with their acres of cleared, rolling countryside, ancient trees, and natural vistas, already existed here, but Nature was, if anything, too raw for comfort, and colonists preferred the order of formal French gardens in their plantings, especially those near the house. America was influenced by the eighteenth-century love of Chinese objects—porcelain, lacquer, wallpaper, and the like—but the mentality of the eighteenth-century French rococo found few sympathetic vibrations here. Chinese fretwork, however, did achieve a certain architectural popularity. The James Reid house (1757), in Charleston, South Carolina, was in the Chinese Taste; Gunston Hall (1758), in Fairfax County, Virginia, and the Miles Brewton house (1769), also in Charleston, were homes with Gothic and Chinese architectural motifs in mouldings and stair railings.[12] Thomas Jefferson, as early as 1771, had the intention to build an eighteenth-century Gothic pavilion in the burial grounds at Monticello,[13] but he contented himself with Chinese fretwork galleries at his home and a serpentine brick wall on the grounds of the University of Virginia. Decorative style in late

eighteenth-century America went directly from a modified English Georgian to neoclassicism. The modern taste of Louis XV rococo was simply bypassed until the mid-nineteenth-century revival of that style.

During the time that the new republic was actively engaged in the work of creating its government, it was also at work, at the social level, refining and polishing an adult image of itself. The niceties and restrained pace of life in the neoclassical mode were felt to have an ennobling and a civilizing effect upon our somewhat uncouth population. America's federal and state government buildings, important business houses, and Eastern domestic architecture took on the look of Greece and Rome; beneath the idealized surface of this adopted identity, however, there were romantic stirrings. The published admiration of European visitors for our natural scenery brought many tourists to our wilderness areas. Beginning in the 1820s, America produced some native voices: James Fenimore Cooper, Washington Irving, John James Audubon, and the Hudson River painters.

The Romantic Forest

The visual romance of the forest depends a great deal on light—the breaking-up of space with light into an infinity of pattern. Nature's unceasing latticework interrupts the course of light to produce silhouettes and shadowy voids. The only flat planes in the forest are quiet pools of water and flat rocks. The forest is growing; it has movement and energy. It also seems to stand still and rest in the deep shade of great, slow-growing trees and in the dim light and coolness of natural rock grottoes. Most significantly, the sense of self and the hard edges of individuality become slightly blurred by the multiplicity of forms and the awareness of the large scale and the great antiquity of such a setting. The individual momentarily joins hands with the dust motes drifting slowly down to the forest floor in a diagonal shaft of sunlight, the source of which is so high above the intermediate shade as to be mystical. This is an atmosphere that the painters of the Hudson River school painted again and again, for fifty years, in the nineteenth century—Celtic magic in the primeval forest.

Fig. 2-4. A view of the dramatic scenery above the Natural Bridge of Virginia, from *Picturesque America*, a subscription series of highly romantic American scenic wood engravings. Issued monthly from 1872 to 1874 by D. Appleton and Co., the series was accompanied by a text edited by William Cullen Bryant. (Photo: Courtesy of Lipscomb Library, Randolph-Macon Woman's College)

ABOVE THE NATURAL BRIDGE.

The back-to-Nature theme in America was expressed in many different areas of the East Coast around 1820. The deeper romantic attitudes toward Nature were closer to European attitudes in the Hudson River valley region near New York City (see fig. 2-5), but the fashionable eighteenth-century picturesque styles in architecture and rustic work appeared slightly earlier in the South. Jefferson's plans for a "a gothic temple" (never completed) in 1804 and his ordering of the bricks for its construction in 1807 show his preoccupation with the picturesque.[14] Both Jefferson and John Adams made extensive tours of the English parks while they were together in England in 1786.

The Virginia Springs

Picturesque architecture and rustic furniture in the South are inseparably linked with the social history of summer recreation in the nineteenth century. The memory of stifling summer heat without air conditioning has, by now, faded for at least two generations of Americans. In former days in the South, where the heat of summer was most oppressive, high ceilings, white clothing, lavender water, hand fans, and mint juleps were so much a part of the summer that today any one of these objects stands as a metaphor for life in that region of the country. The only escape from the humid heat and the "miasma" was, for those who could afford it, removal either to the seacoast or to the

Fig. 2-5. Naive watercolor drawing, *The Memory Lesson*, by Sophia Hamilton (active New York state, ca. 1820). In addition to the rustic settee in the garden foreground, there is an indistinctly drawn bench near the gardener in the right mid-ground. (Photo: Courtesy of the Museum of Fine Arts, Boston, M. and M. Karolik Collection)

mountains, and because of the incidence of cholera and malaria on the coast, more often it was to the mountains.

Beginning in the 1750s, when Newport, Rhode Island, was still just a colonial town and a collection of small farms, Southern planters from the West Indies and the coasts of the Carolinas and Virginia removed their families each summer to Newport via sailing ships. Saratoga Springs, near Albany, New York, later claimed a number of annual visitors from the South. The Virginia Springs resorts in the western mountains of Virginia began to evolve in 1750. By 1808, there were nine well-established mineral spas in this region, all but one of them within a radius of sixty miles of the White Sulphur Springs in what is now southern West Virginia.

These cool summer resorts with their healing springs attracted affluent visitors by the hundreds. Because many of the families from the plantation areas of the South lived at remote distances from one another, not the least of the Springs' attractions was the opportunity they provided for courtship among young men and women of similar social backgrounds. In many ways, the Virginia Springs became self-perpetuating annual family reunions. Additionally, not a little of the business and government of the United States was conducted each summer at the Springs.

The Springs attracted patrons from all over the South and the Eastern Seaboard. Given the incredible difficulty of reaching the area, even after the completion of the James River and Kanawha Turnpike in 1824, that they made the lengthy journey at all tells us the importance of the resorts to the people of the day. In *Letters Descriptive of the Virginia Springs, The Roads Leading Thereto, and the Doings Thereat* (1835), "Peregrine Prolix," commenting upon the condition of the road from Charlottesville into the Warm Springs, wrote:

> In some places, to the inexperienced, it has an awfully dangerous appearance, running up the side of a steep mountain, and having no parapet wall. The safety, however, lies in the horses, who cannot by any means be persuaded to run off the road.[15]

The hotels, at first, comprised a collection of log cabins surrounding the Springs. These were superseded by large, handsome stone, brick, or wooden hotel buildings. Many of the cabins, as well as new "cottages," took care of the overflow. (William Lewis, the proprietor of The Sweet Springs, used the courthouse and the jail to house guests in the crowded summer seasons of the 1830s.) The cottages very quickly became more desirable than the overfilled hotel buildings. The term *cottage* was thenceforth used to describe any unattached summer home, from a small board-and-batten *cottage ornée* to a 200-room

Renaissance chateau. The architectural style of the hotel buildings was American Georgian, with some adumbrations here and there of the popular Greek revival.

With respect to landscape design, however, the natural lines of the particular mountain valley were preserved. Attractive picturesque paths and walks through the virgin forests were cleared and "seats made of logs" were provided along the forest paths for rest and for leisurely conversation. No one ever seems to have been in a hurry at the Springs. Early nineteenth-century visitors' descriptions of the scene give a consistent picture of languid tranquillity and simple pleasure amidst the beauty and harmony of Nature.[16]

"Charleston in the Mountains"

Foreign naturalists and botanists in search of exotic flora and fauna had been entering the Appalachians through old Indian trails since the eighteenth century. In the early 1800s, amateur tourists, also, were examining the mountain scenery from comfortable, but increasingly crowded bases at the Springs.

In 1817, a group of five socially prominent men from Charleston discovered Flat Rock in North Carolina, some twenty-five miles southeast of Asheville. A land grant containing over a thousand acres for each family was obtained in 1820.[17] The colony at Flat Rock became a summer extension of cosmopolitan Charleston, sheltering not only native Charlestonians, but also foreign consuls from France, Germany, and England. Flat Rock borrowed its architecture and its furniture from the latest English fashion—the picturesque. There were Jacobean gatehouses, Gothic pavilions, Italian villas, the usual racetracks, and deer parks. After the completion of the Buncombe Turnpike in 1827, the summer population increased enough to support the construction of an Episcopalian chapel at Flat Rock, later taken under the guidance of Bishop L. Silliman Ives of North Carolina. One of the earliest surviving pieces of rustic furniture in the mountains owes its genesis to the social and religious attitudes of the colony at Flat Rock.

Valle Crucis Abbey

After some years of utopian religious planning, an Episcopal mission was established in a remote mountain region near Boone, North Carolina. Valle Crucis (Vale of the Cross) Abbey was begun in 1842 by Bishop Ives and two other Episcopal priests from New York. (Ives' wife was the daughter of the Episcopal Bishop of New York.) Named for the old Valle Crucis Abbey in Denbighshire, Wales, the mission was the first attempt since the Reformation to establish an Anglican religious order. We must assume, from the beginning, that Bishop Ives was heavily influenced by the Cambridge Camden Society and the Anglican Tractarians associated with the Oxford Reform Movement of the 1830s. This movement in the Anglican Church was an effort to revive religious enthusiasm by reaching back to the color and emotional pageantry of the early liturgical forms of the Church (stopping just short of Rome).[18] It was a highly romantic movement, which, among other things, permanently welded Gothic architecture to the Anglican Church.

The mission established a school and a chapel in this secluded region of the mountains and promptly set about to convert the natives. Drawing on local mountaineers as communicants, students, and candidates for the priesthood, the abbey struggled along. By 1849, dark rumors drifting from the mountains had it that the abbey was becoming "a feeble and undignified imitation of the monastic institutions of the Church of Rome."[19] Both the Church and a United States senator investigated. The rumors were true. According to the Church, Bishop Ives, owing to a fever in 1848, in the course of which he lost a certain "mental poise," and also from the fact that there was "insanity in his family," had "tolerated the Romish notion of the Invocation of Saints, Auricular Confession and Absolution," but he had drawn the line just before the doctrine of transubstantiation.[20] Bishop Ives signed a paper to this effect; the Order was disbanded; and then, in 1852, the bishop journeyed to Rome and committed "the Apostasy of converting to the Roman Church,"[21] only a few years after the Tractarian John Henry Newman had done a similar thing.

In 1844, another man came to Valle Crucis, and stayed. William West Skiles, in every way the polar opposite of Bishop Ives, was a carpenter, interestingly enough. A native of the North Carolina coast, he was hired to take charge of the agricultural department of Valle Crucis. Skiles became, in rapid succession, the chief carpenter, engineer, and practical manager of the abbey, and then a lay reader and an ordained deacon. In effect, Skiles ran the abbey. The only one of the monks to retain his vows after the abbey was disbanded, he remained in the region as a teacher, preacher, postmaster, and doctor. Until his death in 1862, he was one of the most beloved men in the mountains.

Among the buildings at the abbey was a chapel that served the community. On the left-hand side of the chancel reposed a rustic bishop's chair, dating from 1847. In 1890, Susan Fenimore Cooper, the daughter of James Fenimore Cooper, wrote a loving memoir of Brother Skiles and the missionary life at Valle Crucis. In a footnote on the origin of the bishop's chair, she wrote: "The Bishop's Chair, ingeniously constructed out of Laurel by a member of the Mission (Rev. Mr. Bland) still may be seen at Valle Crucis, a

Fig. 2-6. The bishop's chair from Valle Crucis Abbey (1847), rhododendron; the bishop's mitre is carved of the same wood. (Photo: John Mast)

Fig. 2-7. Rhododendron chair (date unknown) from the chancel of the church at Valle Crucis. (Photo: John Mast)

valued relic."[22] In 1847, Mr. Bland would have been one of the young mountaineer candidates for ordination. The chair (fig. 2-6) is now in a stone chapel at Valle Crucis; two other old, but undated, chairs of rhododendron can be seen in the chancel. (Fig. 2-7)

The bishop's chair is an eye-catcher and certainly one of the most extraordinary pieces of ecclesiastical furniture in the United States. One suspects that the prototype of the chair was a hall chair in an English Gothic *cottage ornée*, but for all its presumably sincere religious expression, there is more than a hint of the darkly comic about it. Is the chair a grotesque satire on the state of affairs at Valle Crucis and, if so, was it conscious or unconscious? Could a young divinity student, perceiving the sharp differences between a troubled, idealistic "citizen" bishop and a deeply sincere, practical "rustic" deacon build for his bishop a cathedral seat that expresses that discrepancy so perfectly? We do not know, but it is the consensus of all who view the chair that it is neither beautiful nor is it entirely ugly.

Andrew Jackson Downing and the Picturesque in America.

The tastemaker *par excellence* in nineteenth-century America was the landscape designer Andrew Jackson Downing (1815–1852). The highly respected editor of *The Horticulturist* magazine, Downing was best known for two architectural stylebooks: *Cottage Residences* (1842) and *The Architecture of Country Houses* (1850). Written in collaboration with the architects Alexander Jackson Davis and Calvert Vaux, both books went through several editions.

In the 1840s and 1850s, the United States was confronted, for the first time, with "the urban problem." The agrarian values upon which America had been founded underwent severe stress as the Industrial Revolution and heavy immigration poured thousands of people into cities. At the time, the cities were regarded with hostility by all but the most aggressively avaricious businessmen. It was Downing's major

Fig. 2-8. Design VIII for a bracketed *cottage ornée*. Andrew Jackson Downing, *The Architecture of Country Houses* (1850). Compare this design with the cottage in fig. 2-3.

Fig. 2-9. Rustic summerhouse. Andrew Jackson Downing, *Cottage Residences* (1844).

achievement to effect a satisfactory compromise between the city and the country. He considered the city a necessary evil; but virtue, he felt, could thrive only in a rural setting. Downing singlehandedly invented the picturesque suburb in America. Halfway between the impersonal wheels of commerce and the too rough, uncivilized wilderness, Downing designed homes for people in idyllic natural surroundings beyond the city limits. The suburb remained within reach of the city via the new railroads.

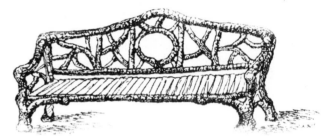

Fig. 2-10. Rustic settee. Andrew Jackson Downing, *Cottage Residences* 4th ed. (1852).

Fig. 2-11. Cottage for a country clergyman, showing rustic porches and decoration. Andrew Jackson Downing, *Cottage Residences* 4th ed. (1852).

DESIGN XI.
A COTTAGE FOR A COUNTRY CLERGYMAN.

View in the Grounds of James Arnold. Esq.

Fig. 2-12. Rustic tree seat and summerhouse. Andrew Jackson Downing, *A Treatise on the Theory and Practice of Landscape Gardening Adapted to North America* 4th ed. (1849).

ORNAMENTAL ICE HOUSE ABOVE GROUND.

Fig. 2-13. An ice house showing rustic brackets. Andrew Jackson Downing, *Rural Essays* (1858).

ORNAMENTAL ICE HOUSE ABOVE GROUND.

Fig. 2-14. Thatched ice house, walls covered with mosaic twigwork or, perhaps, bark veneer held in place with patterned half-round twigs. Andrew Jackson Downing, *Rural Essays* (1858). (For a description of bark mosaics on the walls of summerhouses, see J. C. Loudon, *Encyclopedia of Cottage, Farm and Villa Architecture*, 1832, p. 986.)

Hundreds and thousands, formerly obliged to live in the crowded streets of cities, now find themselves able to enjoy a country cottage, several miles distant,—the old notions of time and space being half annihilated; and these suburban cottages enable the busy citizen to breathe freely, and keep alive his love for nature, till the time shall come when he shall have wrung out of the nervous hand of commerce enough means to enable him to realize his ideal of the "retired life" of an American landed proprietor.[23]

Downing was responsible, too, for the nineteenth-century *rus in urbe*, the city park. It was only after his tragic death in a steamboat accident that his plans for Central Park in New York City were realized by the landscape architect Frederick Law Olmstead, who took on Downing's assistant, Calvert Vaux, as a partner.

As his drawings will show, Downing borrowed his plans from England. The rustic country-box, the Swiss chalet, the Gothic house, the Italian villa—all of these dwellings were reworked to include several of Downing's ideas on the use of native materials and specific adaptations for America. He labored long, in print and on the drawing board, to provide esthetically pleasing homes for the common people of America. Downing was particularly fond of the English picturesque, and his books are full of engravings and woodcuts of cottage-style rustic work—settees, chairs, summerhouses, Gothic entryways, and vine-covered rustic porches. (Figs. 2-8 through 2-14) The cast-iron-work on porches, so popular in America and an early nineteenth-century development in England and France, had its origins in the rustic work of hermitages and the vine-covered Gothic porches of the *cottage orñee*. (See fig. 2-15.)

Downing's efforts to popularize architectural taste were immediately successful. Fredrika Bremer mentions in *Homes of the New World* (1853) that his books were "to be found everywhere, and nobody, whether he be rich or poor, builds a house or lays out a garden without consulting Downing's work."[24] Philadelphia diarist Sidney George Fisher wrote: "The influence of Downing's work is seen everywhere in buildings and grounds. . . . He has done a vast deal of good

Fig. 2-15. Cast iron *treillage*. Edward S. Brown house, Lynchburg, Virginia, 1884.

in reforming the style of country residences and suggesting new and beautiful embellishments."[25] Downing's picturesque cottages and vertical board-and-batten Gothic-style houses were used frequently for summer homes. His rustic furniture was used in parks, picturesque gardens, and on many, many porches. It was the height of country-in-the-town fashion.

The Gothic revival in England, particularly as it related to various ecclesiastical revivals in liturgical and architectural forms, was a strong influence on this style in America. The Episcopal clergy in the Northeast, moving in and out of the wealthy social circles of New York, together with the Anglican society of certain Southern planters, managed to transmit the Gothic taste far and wide—even to areas unaware of the current philosophical, religious, and moral significance of the Gothic. Susan Fenimore Cooper explained the picturesque religious scene at Valle Crucis: "The good people learned the chants and anthems, and took pleasure in singing them in their rude, but kindly homes. Little bands of men and women, [after a Sunday service] would often go on their way through the forest paths chanting the Benedicite—a holy song of praise never before heard in those ancient forests. And these were people who could not read."[26] (Doubtless, the "good people" played the holy tunes on their dulcimers, too—instruments tuned to church modes far older than the nineteenth-century High Church tonality of the *Benedictus.*) The New York architect Richard Upjohn, in the forties and fifties, designed a number of small wooden Gothic churches and offered the designs free to Episcopal congregations in rural areas.

For many reasons, reform in morals and taste was the favorite parlor game of a great many eminent Victorians. There is a tone of genuine concern for the welfare of people, and also for the intelligent conservation of the land, in Andrew Jackson Downing's work, which probably accounts for his success, but "tiresome cant" and "pious knavery" characterized many of the social parlors and not a few of the rectories of New York City. Nevertheless, this social, religious, and political elite, socializing together in the summer months, laboring together in the winter, did succeed in establishing a widespread architectural fashion, derived, in part, from the styles of their own summer hermitages.

The Victorian Era in England

The immense popularity of cottage rustic garden structures—small pavilions and summerhouses, aviaries, ice houses, pergolas, and the like—which acquired momentum from the 1840s onward, accounts for the continued use of the picturesque furniture. The Fox-Talbot calotype reproduced as figure 2-16, an extremely early photograph, shows a mother seated on a rustic bench and her children near the rustic lattice of a summerhouse. Beginning around 1844, the magazine *Punch* introduced drawings of rus-

Fig. 2-16. William Henry Fox-Talbot calotype, dated 19 April 1842, showing a summerhouse with a rustic Gothic porch having two facing seats on the interior. The woman is seated on a rustic Gothic stool.

tic work (figs. 2-17 and 2-18), and the rustic twigwork initial letters, so much a stylistic feature of *Punch*, made their first appearance. The world's first Christmas card, drawn by John Calcott Horsley for Sir Henry Cole in 1843, was decorated with a rustic grapevine and a rustic Gothic banner bearing the greeting. Illustrators of children's books in the 1870s were partial to the quaint rustic style. Figure 2-19 shows an English settee from the Edwardian era.

John Steegman in *Victorian Taste* points out that in England, beginning in the 1840s, the increased inter-

MR. JOHN BULL IN HIS WINTER GARDEN

Fig. 2-18. Cartoon showing "John Bull" in his glass conservatory, seated on a rustic stool studying *Paxton's Flower Garden*. A few members of the "great unwashed" can be seen on the outside looking in. *Punch* (vol. XXI, 1851, p. 79).

Fig. 2-17. Rustic alligator bench from the magazine *Punch* (vol. VI, 1844, p. 230). If the tall tail were fitted with pegs to serve as hangers for toys or clothes, this bench would make a novel item for a child's room.

Fig. 2-19. An English rustic settee from the Edwardian era.

est in gardening and the abundant use of cut flowers and potted plants indoors heralded the revival of the exuberant, colorful, and rich decoration of the rococo revival of the 1850s.[27] Joseph Paxton's Crystal Palace, housing the Great Exhibition of 1851, demonstrated a means of bringing the garden indoors by the use of glass. French windows, verandas, and conservatories opened the Victorian home to the color of the flower garden just outside. If the eighteenth century removed garden walls to admit mood-producing vistas of land, trees, and sky, the nineteenth century created apertures in the walls of their houses to admit the forms and color of flowers.

We have said that ornamental style is a double-faced screen, guarding against, yet expressing, new cultural tendencies—a symbolic working-out of the adjustment between old and new. The consequences of the many imaginative leaps forward in technology, science, and social theory that had been unleashed by the eighteenth century and the Industrial Revolution had, somehow, to be assimilated and integrated into the social fabric of the culture. The cultural tasks confronting the Victorians seem to have frightened them into blind seriousness in almost every pursuit. There was little energy left over for graceful, humorous play for the sake of play. Where the Devil seems to have a real presence, society cannot afford to flirt with him.

The underlying fear seems to have been that of cultural annihilation. For reassurance, the Victorians turned to Nature; moreover, to the proof of the fertility of Nature—her flowers. Unlike the gardeners of the eighteenth century, who were somewhat indifferent to flowers, the nineteenth century gardeners adored flowers. Not only did they cultivate indoor and outdoor gardens, they also wove flowers into their carpets, wallpapered rooms with them, carved naturalistic furniture, and decorated every available blank space on wood, stone, metal, pottery, canvas, and fabric with vine, tendril, leaf, and flower, not to mention filling their houses with the sight and scent of cut flowers. In a chapter on grotesque art of the Renaissance in *The Stones of Venice* (1851–1853), John Ruskin wrote:

> . . . in the utmost solitude of nature, the existence of Hell seems to me as legibly declared by a thousand spiritual utterances, as that of Heaven. It is well for us to dwell with thankfulness on the unfolding of the flower . . . and the sleep of the green fields in the sunshine; but the blasted trunk, the barren rock, the moaning of the bleak winds, the roar of the black, perilous, merciless whirlpools, of the mountain streams, the solemn solitudes of moors and seas, the continual fading of all beauty into darkness, and of the strength into dust, have these no language for us? . . . birth and death, light and darkness, heaven and hell, divide the existence of man and his Futurity.[28]

These are powerful images of an "all-or-nothing" struggle. Being a Victorian was not an easy matter. Ruskin tells us that ". . . he whose heart is at once fixed upon heaven, and open to the earth, so as to apprehend the importance of heavenly doctrines, and the compass of human sorrow, will have little disposition for jest."[29]

Looking at the other side of the screen, we can see that the Victorian age was excited and stimulated by the positive effects of the new scientific discoveries and inventive technology. Horticulture, wedding practical science to esthetics, became a stylish psychological playing field for science, art, and sociology. The Victorians turned the garden "into a school for moral precepts,"[30] although not for the first time.

Among several books published in the 1850s on rustic garden ornament, *Rustic Adornments for Homes of Taste*, by Shirley Hibberd, is of interest. The book is a suffocating moral treatise on the flower garden in which precise rubrics for "enjoyment" are assigned to each border, bank, pond, and "fragrant rustic bower." The emphasis is not on the passive enjoyment of sight and scent, but instead upon the active moral attitude that the viewer is *ordered* to summon up in response to such-and-such an arrangement of colorful plants and rustic work. The twentieth-century reader is bewildered by Hibberd's bland assumptions and tone of authority—the words are English, but it is another language—and yet, the first London edition in 1856 sold out in six months, a second edition in 1857 was soon out of print as well, and a third, enlarged edition of 1870 sold out promptly. In addition to its popularity in England, the book became the focus of attention in America in the struggle for international copyright laws. In 1862, a book called *Rand's Flowers for the Parlor and Garden*, published in Boston, copied many of the woodcuts and utilized a good bit of Mr. Hibberd's text without due credit. Rand's book went through three editions before it came to the attention in 1867 of the new political journal, *The Nation*. In two separate articles[31] (written most probably by Frederick Law Olmstead),[32] *The Nation* devoted some nine columns of its rather limited space to exposing the plagiarism. Plagiarism notwithstanding, both books enjoyed six or seven printings each in America.

According to his remarks in the Preface of his book, Mr. Hibberd proposed "to enlarge the circles of domestic pleasures and home pursuits . . . to quicken observation of natural phenomena, so that the meanest of familiar things shall become eloquent in praise of beneficence and beauty; to strengthen family ties and affections. . . ." The "recreations" Hibberd was about to impart to the reader were designed "to help the soul in its aspirations by conducting it away from disturbing scenes, and surrounding it with an atmosphere of health and peacefulness."

There are several designs in the book for Gothic-style rustic summerhouses, complete with stained glass windows. Mr. Hibberd regarded the rustic summerhouse as *de rigueur* in the well-appointed garden, but his little hermitages are neat as a pin and so orderly in their construction that no "Goth" could ever recognize them. Rustic work had ceased to be rustic; wild nature had been tamed, not to say chopped down and sat upon. All the same, it was still present in the garden.

Several rustic settees are shown in Hibberd's book, all of them similar to those of A. J. Downing. Hibberd is very thorough in his description of specific details in the use of plants, and, as a matter of moral course, he lists the titles of certain inspirational books to be included in the summerhouse library. But apart from warning against dry rot in the rustic oak and the use of nondrying varnishes on the settees, he gives no technical information on the construction of these objects.

If there is a single outstanding contrast between the eighteenth century and the nineteenth century, it must lie with attitudes toward visual perception. The nineteenth century contracted its domestic field-of-vision, even to the point of studying Nature through the lens of a microscope. In the words of the redoubtable Mr. Hibberd, the soul was to be helped in its aspirations "by conducting it away from disturbing scenes." The scenes *were* disturbing. England's population had tripled during the eighteenth century, and a growing part of that population was concentrated in cities. In the nineteenth century, England moved some of its teeming multitudes to other lands.

The Victorians contracted the space of gardens as well; they tended small lawns planted with colorful, patterned "carpet gardens," rather like the bedded plants that can be seen today in European parks. The wall was rebuilt on the far side of the garden, while the garden was observed through the panes of transparent glass. What could not be reformed and made to seem "beneficent" beyond the garden wall did not have to be seen. Little by little, beginning around 1850, English gardeners began to create again the formal Italian parterre; finally, in the late 1880s, the picturesque was condemned for its irregularity.

Because of the American Revolution, the arrival of the picturesque on this side of the Atlantic was delayed. And, in the nineteenth century, its presence in America extended over a longer period of time. The widespread revival of eighteenth-century style was not clearly evident in America until around 1910–1915.

As communication techniques evolved during the nineteenth century, however, America was subject to many overlapping European style trends. By 1900, it was possible to find a little of everything in the United States.

The Nineteenth-Century Resorts

In the 1830s and 1840s, rustic summerhouses and garden seats could be found from Baltimore to Boston in the Northeast. The Hudson River region around Tarrytown, New York, an early enclave of the English picturesque Gothic, borrowed wooden rustic work and cast-iron seats from English models. Washington Irving designed a particularly successful iron seat in the Gothic style.[33] Landscaped park-cemeteries—"a distinctively American contribution to the art of gardens"[34]—such as Spring Grove in Boston, employed rustic seats, and suburban estates on Long Island and in New Jersey copied English rustic summerhouses and garden ornaments. Alexander Jackson Davis and Andrew Jackson Downing, as we have mentioned, promulgated the fashion that was much used in both the coastal and inland resorts, as well as in suburban gardens. Frederick Law Olmstead considered rustic work to be well adapted for city parks.

In the sixties and seventies, rustic furniture found increasing competition from wicker furniture, made at first of rattan and willow wrapped on a steam-bent framework of slender hickory and white oak poles.[35] By the 1870s the fancy American wicker furniture,

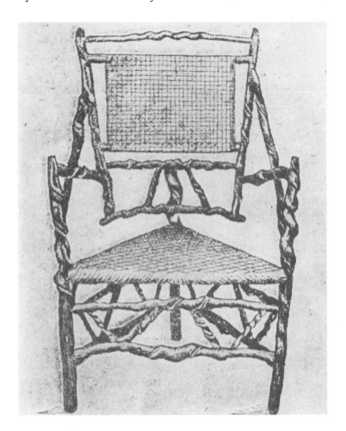

Fig. 2-20. Victorian chair. The triangular legs hark back to chairs from the Middle Ages. The form of this chair (but not its rustic material) was cited in an article in *The House Beautiful* (August 1916, p. 146) as an example of "bad taste."

with its rococo curves, bulges, and curlicues, was being used indoors and out. Some of the sturdy grotesque furniture altered its shape to accommodate Victorian taste. (Fig. 2-20) The majority of all rustic furniture, however, in both the Northeast and in the South, was constructed for and used in summer resorts.

Cleveland Amory mentions in *The Last Resorts* an old theory of the natural progression of diverse groups of people at summer resorts:

> First, artists and writers in search of good scenery and solitude; second, professors and clergymen and other so-called "solid people" with long vacations in search of the simple life; third, "nice millionaires" in search of a good place for their children to lead the simple life (as lived by the "solid people"); fourth, "naughty millionaires" who wished to associate socially with the "nice millionaires" but who built million-dollar cottages and million-dollar clubs, dressed up for dinner, gave balls, and utterly destroyed the simple life; and fifth, trouble. [36]

With a few exceptions, this "Gresham's Law of Resorts" holds true for the entire summer-resort phenomenon. The nineteenth century seethed with activity among various social groups seeking a picturesque, cool, and, above all, exclusive resorting spot.

At the same time that early nineteenth-century tourists were active in the South, the great coastal and inland resorts of the North—Bar Harbor, Newport, Cape May, Long Branch, Nahant, and areas in the Berkshires, the White Mountains, and the Poconos— were under development. The picturesque Gothic cottages of A. J. Downing and A. J. Davis were everywhere and the country craftsmen were kept busy supplying cottages with rustic furniture.

In the 1850s, the North and the South began to withdraw to their respective regions. Southern resorters developed private areas near the old spas, and they continued to penetrate into other regions in the North Carolina, Tennessee, and Virginia mountains. The economic devastation of the South following the Civil War caused the closing of all but the largest and most popular of the Springs; by the end of the sixties, however, aided by the coming of the railroads into the mountains, most of the resorts were again filled to capacity.

By that time, too, the resorts of the North were filling up with "nice" millionaires and several "naughty" ones. Along with dressing up for dinner and observing other decorous social conventions, the newly rich industrial resorters invariably carried with them a hair-trigger form of social indignation to use as a weapon against all other parvenus. One slight deviation from their rigid rules of social protocol was enough to ostracize the newcomer.

An often repeated anecdote from this era at the White Sulphur Springs will serve to illustrate the underlying attitudes: Mrs. Anna Washington Tucker of Virginia was introduced to a new group of young women on the portico of the hotel. The conversation introduced a new topic—not the degree of family kinship, but the occupations of the girls' fathers. The father of one was a New York investment banker, another ran a meat-packing empire, and one was the president of a steel company. When Mrs. Tucker was asked what her father did, she replied that he was a farmer. Some moments later, after suitable indignation had been expressed privately concerning the fact that a farmer's daughter had been granted the privilege of resorting at "The Old White," the young ladies were told the name of Mrs. Tucker's father's farm. It was Mount Vernon. [37]

The result of this unfortunate social insecurity sent artists, writers, and intellectual "solid people" fleeing in disgust to regions remote from the social resorts. Charles Darwin's *Origin of Species* howled down from the wild and the testing of the survival of the fittest coincided with the flight from the resorts.

The Wilderness Camp

A number of husbands, also, attempted to escape the formality of the resorts in the East; this time not to picturesque Nature, but to the ruggedness of the true wilderness. Beginning in the seventies and eighties and continuing through the early 1900s, a curious rebellion against feminine social tyranny resulted in a large-scale movement that might be called "Man-and-Boy-in-the-Wilderness." The hunting and fishing camps, first built in the 1870s in the Adirondack Mountains of New York, were a part of this reaction against the constraints of the society resorts. From that time on, the term *camp* was used to signify a wilderness retreat, as opposed to a resort cottage.

One aspect of the revival of medievalism in the early nineteenth century was the resurrection of the chivalric idealization of women. Doubtless, the new knights of the Industrial Revolution felt the need of the redeeming, ennobling presence of a good woman. For complex reasons, a fantasy role was assigned to wives and mothers. They were expected to be the keepers of morality, cleanliness, and culture; poorly educated as a group, many of them became the pawns of unctuous clergymen and earnest male reformers. Left to themselves within their carefully defined spheres, they became overbearing and too powerful by far. ("The hand that rocks the cradle/ Is the hand that rules the world," issued forth ambiguously from the pen of Wm. Ross Wallace in the middle of the nineteenth century.) Tom Sawyer was not the only boy to suffer under an Aunt Polly. Perhaps to regain their masculine self-esteem, perhaps only to escape starched collars and party manners in the hot summertime, fathers took their sons and headed off to play Nimrod in the forest.

The many, many books from the period on camp craft, Indian lore, hunting and fishing, survival in the wilderness (largely considered to be a beneficent wilderness), and the children's fiction attest to the strength of the rebellion. The Boy Scouts of America and several other organized wilderness youth groups were established in the early 1900s. Camp life was rugged, romantic, and very rustic. Rustic furniture, in many regions, promptly lost its formal outlines and became crudely functional. Noble savages customarily sit on the lap of Mother Earth.

Where camps were permanent, rather than movable tents, the architecture was rather quickly standardized. Built of round logs, the camps were something of a cross between the older Gothic cottages and Swiss chalets and the hewn log cabins of the American pioneers. Often, the porches of the cabins had rustic Chinese fretwork railings, and pole fences of fretwork enclosed the cabin areas. The fence gate was an elaborate rustic triumphal archway. A wooden sign, into which was burned the name of the camp (Indian, if possible), was posted near the entryway.

Eventually, women were invited to the camps, but the wilderness camp was intimidating to them and, as a rule, they did not stay very long, preferring their fiefdoms at the resorts. Their daughters, however, around 1910, found camp life to be delightful. They adapted themselves to it readily, always remembered to admire the stuffed moose heads and the hornets' nests, and never made the mistake of trying to change the place into more than what it was. The eighteenth-century rustic chair in figure 1-4 would have been as out of place in the wilderness camp setting as a gilded rococo armchair.

"The Third Estate"

From the East, the fashion of summer resorts spread westward. In the 1859 edition of *The Virginia Springs and Springs of the South and West*, by Dr. J. J. Moorman, resident physician at the White Sulphur Springs, some 74 springs were listed—from Virginia to Kentucky, Alabama, Ohio, Arkansas, and New Mexico. In the 1873 edition, Moorman listed 151 springs.

It was the coming of the railroads, especially after the Civil War, that created the widespread vogue of summer resorting among people of more modest means. Small hotels and summer boarding houses sprang up overnight in every cool region or mountain village with a rail stop and a view. The Appalachian Mountains continued to receive the bulk of the summer tourists because of their proximity to the sweltering towns of the coastal plains and piedmont regions. Each summer, entire families came to spend

a week, two weeks, two months in the mountains; accommodations were available to suit a clerk's salary or a millionaire's.

Children and young adults hiked, picnicked, fished, and waded in mountain streams, while grandparents rocked and visited on hotel porches. The demand for chairs was acute. Traditional chairmakers provided ladder-backs and a few Windsors; the chairmakers, and also carpenters, handymen, and farmers, made rustic chairs and swings and settees of rhododendron, hickory, oak, and sometimes, in the 1870s and 1880s, the mountain craftsmen, professional manufacturers, and gypsy bands added French bentwood chairs and tripod tables to their inventory of trade items.

Thomas Henning (1786–1875), a long-lived chairmaker in Lewisburg, West Virginia, near the White Sulphur Springs, supplied "The Old White" with his first order of twelve dozen chairs in 1812. In the 21 March 1867 issue of *The Greenbrier Independent* appears the following advertisement:

CHAIR MAKING
The undersigned returns thanks to the citizens of public generally for the liberality they have extended to him for Sixty-six years in the chair making business. He has removed across the street, opposite his old stand where he is now engaged in making a lot of chairs for Mr. Frazier of the Alum Springs, and hopes to be able to furnish his old customers, and all who may give him a call.

Old Chairs Repaired
County produce of all kinds taken in exchange for work.
—T. Henning

Henning's plank-bottom (Windsor) and, after 1852, split-bottom ladder-back chairs have been documented, but to date his rustic chairs have not, although he is said to have made rustic furniture.

A great deal of rustic furniture made of rhododendron and laurel roots and limbs can be found today in White Sulphur Springs and in nearby Sweet Springs, West Virginia.

The End of the Era

All over America, to-day, people are imitating the conduct and ideals of our fashionable rich society, the so-called "smart set" of the East; and I am convinced that those ideals are false ideals, tragic ideals, and that it is suicidal for America to imitate them. They are not truly American. They are largely an importation from abroad, and they are much more pernicious here than they are in the social systems that originated them.
—Mrs. Phillip Lydig, *Tragic Mansions* (1927)[38]

The background for this statement reaches well back into the nineteenth century, to the time when fashionable America, embarrassed and irritated by constant social criticism from visiting English authors, among other reasons, turned to France to soothe its wounded self-esteem. French manners and style were imported wholesale to America. The alliance of French taste with the manufacturing technology of the Industrial Revolution transformed every household article in America, from kitchen stoves to whatnot stands, into the voluptuous, frilly curves of the French neorococo. Judging from certain entries in the etiquette books of the 1840s, America needed an importation of manners from some source. Not only was there the problem of tobacco juice, spat everywhere, including on parlor carpets, but there was even a dearth of handkerchiefs. Young men were abjured:

> The rising generation of elegants in America are particularly requested to observe that, in polished society, it is not quite *comme il faut* for gentlemen to blow their noses with their fingers, especially when in the street—a practice infinitely more common than refined. [39]

Just after mid-century, wealthy Americans and the Empress Eugénie of France discovered one another. It was a society that was based upon mutual flattery. The empress needed an admiring court, even if it had to be composed of foreigners, and the Americans needed social acceptance.

The effects of this heady European influence can be seen in the 1880s and 1890s at the old Eastern resorts. The resorts changed character. The Gilded Age hungered for an European identity. "Naughty millionaires" gained the upper hand in a noisy, competitive game of social oneupsmanship. Genealogists were kept busy tracing family pedigrees, not to the humble *Mayflower*, but to Charlemagne. Daughters were married off to titled Europeans and sons were sent to Europe and to the Orient to develop cosmopolitan manners and learning. Wealthy Americans, unable to enjoy their European visits without physically possessing everything that they saw, merely collected all that Europe was willing to part with and stored it in colossal Renaissance "cottages" at Newport, Palm Beach, and Asheville. These resort cottages, the constructions that Henry James called "witless dreams" and "white elephants," were reproductions of an architecture that existed in Europe before the arrival of rustic furniture and, consequently, they were bereft of the "forest chair." Rustic furniture was replaced with French basketwork chairs and wrought-iron chairs with wire mesh seats and backs, fancy American wickerwork, rattan chairs from the Orient, and creations of the taxidermists in the form of horn chairs and stools made of elephant and tiger skins (the animals shot on safari by the owner with a fowling piece from Abercrombie and Fitch).

Rustic furniture continued to be made in the hinterlands of America through the 1930s. In fact, it enjoyed a widespread revival beginning around 1900.

The increasing interest in the antique furniture of eighteenth-century England stimulated the revival. During the Depression years, many farmers, gypsies, and even Indians made and sold it beyond their own territories; by 1940, however, the fashion was stone dead. The summerhouse and the picturesque garden were replaced with other styles. The Depression years, the state parks, the automobile, the changing social and economic climate, and the invention of air conditioning introduced new patterns of summer life. The fragments remain in the form of summer camps for children, a few old grand hotels, and rare pieces of nineteenth-century rustic furniture, which can sometimes be seen today in the summer months reposing on the porches of fine old federal and Victorian period houses, especially in the South.

The American Furniture

By the beginning of the 1840s in America, rustic settees were present in fashionable pockets all over the East Coast. Early cast-iron rustic benches, being faithful copies of the wooden rustic work, probably assisted in the spread of the furniture. As we have mentioned, it was already a thriving craft in the southern Appalachian Mountains.

Appalachian Rustic Work

There are four rather distinct style periods of rustic furniture in the Appalachians. The earliest style is that of the Gothic revival, borrowed from England. The styles of second period first appear during, or just after, the Civil War. At this time, the Appalachian chairmakers were relatively free of outside influences and the craftsmen experimented with new styles derived from their own traditional ladder-back chairs. The third period, beginning in the 1870s, might be called the era of rustic basketwork furniture. Made of slender hardwood rods, or of willow, the chair forms seem to have been based upon French basketwork chairs in willow and upon Spanish contour chairs. Finally, a fourth period, discernable around the turn of the century, introduces the copying of eighteenth-century English or American colonial period chairs.

In the 1920s, all four styles of the preceding periods were still being made in the region between Asheville and the Virginia Springs. The dating of individual pieces of rustic furniture is frequently difficult, as is the determination of specific regional origin. This is largely because the craft, as it developed in the Appalachians, was commonly handed down from father to son with most families working exclusively in a given style and a favorite wood. The existence of this practice should serve as a caution against the casual dating of the furniture by style alone. Accurate dating is further complicated by the fact that various other indicators are, in this case, less than fully reliable. The presence of wrought nails, for example, does not necessarily tell us anything about the age of the piece; because of the conservative craft traditions in the mountains, a chairmaker who ran out of nails might simply manufacture his own at a homemade forge. And finally, natural weathering renders the appearance of the wood unreliable as a dating source.

With the exceptions of those of the second period and some specific aspects of design in the third period, the styles were not a part of the indigenous folkcrafts of the mountaineers. The patterns were most probably introduced when urban summer residents provided the craftsmen with pictures to copy. After the Civil War, the styles were spread through the mountains by itinerant chairmakers who followed the summer markets. One such was Joseph Clarence Quinn (1882–1973), the builder of the furniture shown in

figures 2-50 and 2-51 (see page 67). Quinn was born near Asheville, North Carolina. In 1907, he moved his family to Hot Springs, Virginia, where he established a shop. In 1909, he moved on to Sweet Springs, West Virginia, returning a few years later to White Sulphur Springs. E. L. Goodykoontz is another example of the mountain craftsman who followed the resort trade in the area. (Fig. 2-22 shows a settee he made ca. 1918.) Active in the 1920s at the Sweet Chalybeate Springs, near Sweet Springs, he came to the region from Floyd County, Virginia, where he had learned the craft from an uncle. It is safe to say that Goodykoontz made few changes in his uncle's patterns (one of which survives).

The First Period. The settee shown in figure 2-21 is typical of the style common from the 1820s to the 1850s. Compare this settee with the one shown on the porch of A. J. Downing's cottage in figure 2-8.

Fig. 2-21. Rhododendron settee, Abingdon, Virginia, first half of the nineteenth century.

The settee is made of rhododendron, invariably called "laurel" in the mountains. The smaller laurel, or kalmia, named for the Swedish botanist Peter Kalm, who described the genus in the middle of the eighteenth century, is sometimes called "mountain ivy." The great rhododendron and the catawba rhododendron, growing in dense thickets known as hells, reach from twenty to thirty feet [6–9m] in height in shady coves in the Appalachians. The yellow-orange wood is almost indestructible, especially if the bark is left intact. The wood was often used for tool handles. Most, if not all, of the surviving early rustic work in the mountains was made of this material.

Many of the settees of the early period exhibit characteristics of the eighteenth-century root furniture. The attempt to display irregularity and deformity is prominent. (See fig. 2-21, as an example.) Others reflect the style adaptations from the Gothic revival. The Gothic bishop's chair at Valle Crucis Abbey (fig. 2-6) has already been mentioned. The styles of the settee in figure 2-22 and the chairs in figures 2-23 and 2-24 hark back to the Gothic of the 1830s and 1840s.

Fig. 2-22. Rhododendron settee, made by E. L. Goodykoontz, ca. 1918, Alleghany County, Virginia. Dimensions: back posts, 37½ inches [95.2cm]; front posts, 20 inches [50.8cm]; back seat rail, 53½ inches [136cm]; front seat rail, 56½ inches [143.5cm]; seat height, 16½ inches [42cm]; seat depth, 19 inches [48.3cm].

Fig. 2-23. Rhododendron chair, Greenbrier County, West Virginia, late nineteenth or early twentieth century.

The style characteristics of the Gothic may be seen in the diaper pattern of the backs (also a conspicuous feature of the French rococo) and the diagonal supports for the armrests. Note the suggestion of seventeenth-century "wings" on the backs. These wings, originally used for structural support, often are mere ornaments tying the design of the back to the front parts of the seat. When they are absent, the top rail of the back is usually fitted *over* the upright stiles and allowed to protrude a few inches, creating, in some cases, the suggestion of Chinese chair rails. (See the back of the daybed in fig. 6-17, p. 106.)

Fig. 2-24. Laurel wood rocking chair, White Sulphur Springs, West Virginia.

Fig. 2-25. Detail of mosaicwork seat, nailed onto wooden plank in imitation of weaving pattern of rush-bottomed chairs.

The Second Period. The ladder-back "settin' chair" was the most common style of turned chair in the mountains. The Appalachian settlers, about three-quarters of whom were of Scots-Irish descent, with the remaining quarter made up of German, English, Irish, Welsh, and a few other nationalities, used this seventeenth-century chair to the exclusion of almost all other types. The stick-back and hoop-back Windsor chairs were made in some regions during the late eighteenth and early nineteenth centuries; but the rush- or splint-bottomed ladder-backs, often with rockers added, were an emblem of the mountain home. The posts of these chairs, turned on foot-powered pole lathes, were made from billets of white oak, hickory, or ash, which were hand rived in quarter sections. Easy to construct with simple tools, the chairs could be, and often were, made without a lathe. A drawknife or a penknife was used to plane the wood.

Shortly after the Civil War, ladder-back and Windsor captain's chairs, made from slender undebarked sapling poles, appear in the Appalachians. The seats pictured in figures 2-26 and 2-27 are typical. Closer to the traditional mountain folkcrafts of both chairmaking and basketry, these chairs were originally constructed with mortise-and-tenon joints, using green wood posts and seasoned rungs; consequently, many of them have survived harsh weathering and

Fig. 2-26. Hickory captain's chair, Rockbridge County, Virginia (seat missing).

use over the years. The chairs, made of hickory and occasionally of white oak, are durable and among the most comfortable of all rustic seats.

The settee and two chairs shown in figure 6-9 (page 102) were manufactured by the Old Hickory Chair Company of Martinsville, Indiana, a firm that began making rustic furniture in 1890.[40] The manufacturer's name is stamped into the rear legs of the furniture. The table and chair in figure 2-28 were "production made" in North Carolina, ca. 1920.

The Third Period. Sometime in the mid-1870s or early 1880s, two new chair designs surfaced in the Appalachians. Although made in the early 1920s, the chair shown in figure 6-5 (page 100) is an example of the first design.[41] In all likelihood, the chair form was developed from French basketwork chairs in willow. A simple rectangular framework was constructed; curved arm supports and a curved back were then inserted into the frame and locked into position by the tension in the bent rods.

The second chair design has a most interesting history. The rustic prototype is shown in figures 2-29 and 2-30. The original contour design from which the

Fig. 2-28. Hickory chair and table manufactured in North Carolina, ca. 1920.

Fig. 2-27. A set of hickory chairs, North Carolina, late nineteenth century.

rocking chair illustrated developed was most probably a seventeenth-century Spanish or Portuguese chair having a curule base and a one-piece, tooled leather seat and back. In 1819, Thomas Jefferson received two such "Spanish chairs" as a gift from Thomas B. Robertson of New Orleans. Similar leather slingback, or "Spanish steamer chairs" (fig. 2-31), dating from the early nineteenth century, can be found in homes in New Orleans and Natchez.[42]

The contour rustic chair might have been introduced in the mountains around 1880, by Spanish or Portuguese gypsies who, having been exiled to colonies in South America during the sixteenth and seventeenth centuries, began to filter into the United States in the 1860s and 1870s. These gypsy bands are believed to have introduced a specific seventeenth-century Spanish basketweaving technique to the

mountains around 1880.[43] The basket shown in figure 2-32 is an example of the technique: Parallel willow stakes have been inserted into the woven base and bent upward. At the top of the basket sides, the stakes are interlaced and curved downward again, forming a scalloped border. The ends of the rods are woven in and out in a diagonal directed toward the base, where they are fastened off in a foot border. The technique, producing a lattice weave, demonstrates an economical use of the willow rods. There are echoes of this basketry technique in many of the chairs from the third period. It can be seen directly in the back of the settee shown in figure 2-33. The applied decoration on the top back rails of the settee and the chair in figures 2-22 and 2-23 respectively is probably an attempt to provide a scallop border.

In the Appalachians, the bentwood chairs were

Fig. 2-29. Hickory contour chair, Pocahontas County, West Virginia.

Fig. 2-30. Back view of the chair in fig. 2-29.

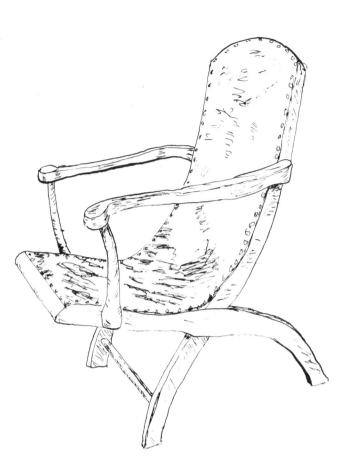

Fig. 2-31. Spanish steamer chair.

Fig. 2-33. Settee from Mountain City, Tennessee, early twentieth century.

Fig. 2-32. Basket from Maryland, ca. 1880, showing Spanish or Portuguese weaving technique.

nearly always constructed of slender young shoots of malleable hardwoods, especially hickory. The pencil-slim saplings, growing in shady coves, rise quickly to reach the light, and ten- to fifteen-foot [3–4.5m] lengths of smooth, one-inch [2.5cm] hickory and white oak are common in Eastern hardwood forests. It is not known whether the style was associated in any direct way with the bentwood beech chairs developed by Michael Thonet in Vienna in the 1840s; nonetheless, there are some intriguing similarities between the shapes of Thonet's chairs and those of the Spanish chairs. It is also known that basket-making techniques from Southern Europe were beginning to spread into Northern Europe at about the same time. William Wrighte's bent apple branch chairs (fig. 2-34) from his stylebook of 1767 show us the early forerunner of Thonet's café chairs. Many bent wire chairs of the early nineteenth century resemble earlier models of rustic chairs, also.

The contour rustic chair was made later with planed seats and backs as shown in figure 2-35. Many such chairs were production-made in the Appalachians beginning around 1890. Figure 2-36 shows an exceptionally fine descendant of the contour rustic rocking chair, manufactured possibly in Pennsylvania. It has been designed with such a positive, artistic refinement that it can scarcely be called rustic, in the sense in which we have been considering the word. The graceful, balanced lines of the chair, the admirable economy

of material, and the functional comfort of the seat are outstanding. Even the problem of blending planed wood with rustic wood has been solved—by separating the planed oak strips of the back to create the necessary space for shadows. (See page 89, for a discussion of the use of shadow as a solution to related design problems.)

The bentwood chair styles became a favorite form of the mountain craftsmen, who made them with dozens of variations for about sixty years. Regardless of the origins of the chairs, the mountaineers considered them their own property and embellished them according to their own ideas of design. There is some significant irony in the fact that neither gypsies nor rural mountaineers had any use for rustic furniture, in general. In most cases, they made it solely for the summer market.

The migration in the mountains of the chair forms of the third period is complicated by the presence of the gypsies. Tracing the gypsies in America is a formidable task, in part because a mythical, often romanticized folklore has attached itself to them. So far as rustic furniture is concerned, the gypsy furniture, as a class, was hastily and poorly constructed and very little of it has survived. Much of what is now called gypsy furniture was actually made in the winter months by native mountaineers and then peddled during the summer, even beyond the mountains. A farmer and his sons, driving a wagon piled high with chairs and tables, would travel to a central town, park the wagon in a safe harbor, load several chairs on the backs of the mules or horses, and then fan out through the area to sell the wares door to door. According to a retired nonagenarian storekeeper in Warm Springs, Virginia, these mountain peddlers were sometimes jokingly referred to as *gypsies*.

There can be little doubt that real gypsies introduced certain forms of tripod tables and willow furniture in the Appalachians, but we cannot, at this point, say with certainty which forms they might be. The tripod table in figure 2-56 and the chair in figure 2-37 have a known gypsy provenance, but since both items are late and the styles they represent were made by such diverse craftsmen as Seminole Indians in Florida and chairmakers from Maine to California, it is not clear who copied from whom. It is likely that gypsies spread many different styles of rustic furniture all over the United States.

Most of the chairs requiring a bending form to set the curves in the green wood (see, for example, the back posts of the chair in fig. 2-30) probably were made by mountaineers. The boxlike framework of the chair in figure 2-37, on the other hand, could have been nailed together by a gypsy chairmaker in a matter of minutes. The factor of time is important since gypsies were seldom permitted to linger for long in any

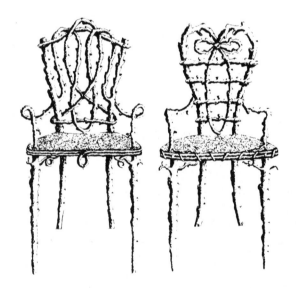

Fig. 2-34. Apple branch chairs from William Wrighte's *Grotesque Architecture, or Rural Amusement* (1767). The chair on the right might have been a design source for Michael Thonet's mid-nineteenth-century café chairs. Note the direction of the buds on the branches; most of the joints have been concealed behind overlapping branches. The front legs have been inverted.

Fig. 2-35. Hickory contour chairs with planed seats and back splats. These are a pair of Mother and Father chairs. Pocahontas County, West Virginia. Purchased in 1920.

Fig. 2-36. Hickory contour rocker with planed white oak seat and back, Greenbrier County, West Virginia. This chair is common throughout the Shenandoah Valley; it appears in summer homes from Highlands, North Carolina, to the Adirondack Mountains.

Fig. 2-37. Gypsy willow chair, Randolph County, West Virginia, ca. 1930.

61

one area, their business practices not being conducive to the development of great trust on the part of the settled populace. Gypsies were primarily attracted to the mountain regions in which the breeding of horses was an important part of the economy; it is still ruefully admitted in the mountains that gypsies were expert judges of fine horses. Greenbrier County, West Virginia, the birthplace of General Robert E. Lee's horse Traveller, saw an annual influx of gypsies from the 1880s until the beginning of World War II.

All of the basketwork chairs of the third period share a number of salient design characteristics. The chairs display a preoccupation with abstract, intricate play with line and an impulse toward restless, tension-filled movement. The eye is drawn immediately into the labyrinthine puzzle of the construction. In fact, upon viewing the chairs, one's first impulse is not to sit in them, but rather to walk around them to study how they are put together. Their rustic simplicity is attractively deceptive; no sooner has one set of lines been traced to its origins than another series breaks in upon one's concentration. Commonly, the furniture is either made up of, or decorated with, slender, actively moving, intermeshed linear elements. The linear character is frequently emphasized by the use of multiple rods of wood. If, in examining

Fig. 2-39. Hickory and maple balloon back contour chair, Jackson County, West Virginia.

Fig. 2-38. Hickory contour chair, Fort Springs, West Virginia, ca. 1890.

Fig. 2-40. Variation on a contour chair, Asheville, North Carolina.

62

figures 2-35 through 2-40, the viewer were to squint slightly, the moving patterns, divorced from their association with chairs, would stand out as a collection of lines. The lines bend back in on themselves, their path is constantly interrupted, but their intricacy is always logical.

Not all of the chairs are well-integrated designs. Some are a hodgepodge of disparate, borrowed ornamentation. In figure 2-39, for example, note the applied Victorian balloon-back decoration (which forms a heart); but see, also, the actively running sine curve of the decoration below the seat. The chair in figure 2-40 is rather awkwardly composed of a square framework and mismatched curvilinear elements, but, again, the spiraling decoration beneath the seat rail draws attention to the impulse for movement.

The chairs in figure 2-41 are a Mother and Father pair. (One of the chairs is slightly smaller than the other; if a child's chair were present in the same group, they would be termed the Three Bears.) The chairs, made of white oak, hickory, and willow, were a wedding present in 1908.

Fig. 2-41. A pair of Mother and Father chairs made of hickory, white oak, and willow, Hillsboro, West Virginia, 1908.

Fig. 2-42. Willow chair, Wautauga County, North Carolina.

When the materials were small enough to be interwoven, weaving patterns were worked into the chairs, as can be seen in the back of the settee in figure 2-33; often, however, woven textures are merely suggested. The chair in figure 2-42 shows the influence of woven wicker furniture.

The back of the chair in figure 2-43 is reminiscent of wrought-iron French Renaissance chairs. The chair has a certain self-conscious "art-student" look about it, and it seems out of place among other mountain chairs.

The Fourth Period. The small laurel doll's chair shown in figure 2-44 and the drawing (fig. 2-45) of a chair made of hickory around 1915 demonstrate another fashion trend: the revival of colonial-style furniture. Chinese Chippendale garden chairs and curved benches in rustic materials, having either stick-back spindles or fretwork, were common through the 1930s. Rustic gazebos, Chinese (and Japanese) curved bridges, and Georgian-style garden structures enjoyed a revival in fashionable suburban homes during this period. The rustic furniture lost its Victorian char-

Fig. 2-43. Bentwood willow chair, Alleghany County, Virginia, ca. 1930.

Fig. 2-44. Chinese Chippendale doll's chair, 14 inches [35.5cm] high. Collected near Rural Retreat, Virginia. Note the deliberate suggestion of a crest rail, the splayed back legs, the basketwork splat and fretwork arm supports, and the brackets supporting the seat rails.

acter and the Chinese look returned. Advertisements in early issues of *The House Beautiful* and *House and Garden* show the popularity of the style.

These Chinese Chippendale styles are seen also in porch swings, as well as in armchairs and benches. They seem to be more common in Virginia than in North Carolina and Tennessee.

The settee in figure 2-46, from New Market, Virginia, made around 1920, has the formal outlines of federal period sofas often found in the Shenandoah Valley. It is dressier than most rustic styles, and it would have been suitable for a colonial-style gazebo made of finished latticework. The somewhat labored decorative circles are unfortunate.

Fig. 2-45. Sketch of a now-damaged rustic chair made of hickory. Shenandoah Valley, ca. 1915.

Fig. 2-46. Hickory and maple settee, New Market, Virginia, ca. 1920.

Case Furniture. In figures 2-47 and 2-48 can be seen some pieces of a rare suite of dining-room furniture, made in the 1930s by one "Reverend" Brown for a family near Penland, North Carolina. In addition to the china cupboard and the sideboard, the group includes a large dining table, twelve chairs, and a side table. The cases are made of pine; the decoration is formed with split pieces of rhododendron and laurel. The original drawer pulls, which have been replaced, were root knobs. Since the design of the individual pieces and the relationships of the individual pieces to the entire suite are perhaps more sophisticated than one might expect from Brown, and since rustic case furniture is unusual in the Appalachians, it is possible that he used pictures of furniture in a catalogue for his models.

Tables and Small Decorative Objects. The table in figure 2-49 is in the Gothic style. Made of debarked saplings, the top was constructed of planed half-logs. Surprisingly, there are no cleats underneath the top; the heavy wood has been joined only with dowels and glue.

Fig. 2-48. China cupboard from Penland, North Carolina.

Fig. 2-47. Sideboard and chair, Penland, North Carolina, 1930s.

66

Figure 2-50 shows a table of rhododendron and laurel made by Joseph Clarence Quinn around 1915. Note the intricate base, the Swiss-work apron, and the rusticated knicks cut into the bark. Mr. Quinn's son, now a retired railroader, mentioned that as a twelve-year-old boy his chief task had been to cut these decorative "rustications" into the stock that his father used to make furniture. Compare this table with the furniture shown in the cartoon from *Punch* in figure 2-18. Quinn also made the doll's furniture in figure 2-51. The table, only four and one-quarter inches [10.8cm] high, is strong enough to stand on. The chair on the left is made of rhododendron, the other pieces are laurel.

Fig. 2-49. Rustic table in the Gothic style, Abingdon, Virginia, first half of the nineteenth century.

Fig. 2-50. Rhododendron and laurel table by Joseph Clarence Quinn, Monroe County, West Virginia, ca. 1915.

Fig. 2-51. Doll's furniture by Joseph Clarence Quinn, White Sulphur Springs, West Virginia, ca. 1920.

The tables shown in figures 2-52 and 2-53, from North Carolina, demonstrate the simplicity of building a rustic table with inverted rhododendron branches. The table tops were made from sections of well-seasoned tree trunk; there are few seasoning cracks.

In figure 2-54 is shown a pitcher made from seasoned rhododendron bole. The cavity, a cylindrical bore, was made with an auger, and the spout was carved with a penknife. Rustic lamp bases also were made in this fashion, as was the cylindrical cigarette container with its lid shown in figure 2-55.

The tripod table made from sassafras wood (fig. 2-56) is of gypsy manufacture, ca. 1919. The tripod plant stand (fig. 2-57) was made by a mountain craftsman. These two tables illustrate the fundamental differences between the gypsy and the mountaineer style of expression. The mountain work was more carefully constructed and the intricacy of pattern was more highly elaborated and sought after. Gypsy work was constructed with casual abandon, with only slight attention paid to details. In fact, the chair in figure 2-40 is so characteristic of the gypsy mode of work that I seriously question the informant who assured me that a distant member of her family had made the chair.

Fig. 2-53. Rustic table, North Carolina. (The candle stands on the table are made from gourds.)

Fig. 2-52. Rustic table bases and stool, North Carolina.

Fig. 2-54. Grotesque pitcher made of rhododendron bole by E. L. Goodykoontz, Old Sweet Springs, West Virginia, ca. 1920.

Fig. 2-56. Gypsy tripod "fern stand," Bath County, Virginia, ca. 1924.

Fig. 2-55. Cigarette box, rhododendron, North Carolina.

Fig. 2-57. Hickory tripod fern stand made by a mountain craftsman, Abingdon, Virginia, ca. 1895.

Fig. 2-58. Art Deco tripod table in willow, Abingdon, Virginia, 1930s.

Fig. 2-59. Willow "smoking table," Kingsport, Tennessee, 1930s.

The "corduroy" tabletop in figure 6-4 (page 99) was uncommon in the Appalachians until around 1920. Usually, tabletops were made of planed wood and edged with strips of rustic half-round molding, or aprons of vertical Swiss work.

Figure 2-58 shows a so-called gypsy tripod table with art deco ornament; the design of the portable table of willow in figure 2-59 seems to have been derived from that of a machine-made "smoking" table. Both pieces date from the 1930s, but no other information concerning their origins is available.

Rustic Furniture in the Adirondack Mountains

The largest collection of American rustic furniture, ca. 1880–1940, is now in the Adirondack Museum at Blue Mountain Lake, New York. Locally made rustic work as well as rustic furniture from the Appalachian Mountains and late nineteenth- and early twentieth-century factory-made ware is contained in the Adirondack collection.

Beginning in the 1870s, a number of New York City sportsmen built permanent summer camps in the wilderness regions of the Adirondacks. The mixture of Swiss chalet and Gothic architectural forms of the camps required its complementary rustic furniture. A great deal of the Adirondack rustic furniture seems to have been made by the same carpenters who built the camps. Inexperienced as furniture makers, their work has a stiff, controlled look to it. The evidence of the carpenter's steel square is everywhere present in carefully mitered corners, compulsively neat geometrical patterns of mosaic twigwork, and in the rigidity of curves. Unable to free themselves from the discipline of machined wood and the rules of carpentry, the builders permitted very little free expressiveness of line or natural form in the furniture. Compared with the freeform romance of the Appalachian rustic work, most of the native Adirondack furniture has an incongruous classical appearance.

The corner cabinet in figure 2-60 is a planed copy of a colonial cupboard, complete with cornice, whose rusticity is supplied with an applied decoration of mosaic twigwork. Made of split half-round twigs in several different colored woods, the geometric patterns were borrowed from simple Indian weaving patterns. The cherry baskets on the doors are a quilt pattern motif common in the nineteenth century. Mosaic twigwork is a notable feature of some of the Adirondack furniture. It is sometimes referred to as "Swiss work" by mid-nineteenth-century English designers, but it is not clear whether the term derives

Fig. 2-60. Rustic corner cupboard featuring mosaic twigwork, late nineteenth century. (Photo: Courtesy of the Adirondack Museum, Blue Mountain Lake, New York)

from the appearance of the closely stacked logs of the Swiss chalet or from the half-round vertical logs in the fascia under the roof of some chalets. Nonetheless, the technique was adapted in England as a solution to the difficult style problem of blending planed and rustic woods. (See page 89 for a practical discussion of the problem.)

The seat in figure 2-61 is a copy of a late-Victorian settee or swing. Once again, the geometrical patterns are very simple, painstakingly constructed, and the entire piece is under rigid geometrical control. "Camp Uncas," worked into the seat in script, is an original touch.

Craig Gilborn, director of the Adirondack Museum at Blue Mountain Lake, has provided the following information on the well-known Adirondack chair, one of which is pictured in figure 2-62: The chair was made about 1914 by Harry C. Bunnell of Westport, New York, who had taken out a patent on this type of porch and lawn chair in 1905 after having seen similar rustic chairs made by a Boston family for their personal use at a camp on Lake Champlain. Mr. Bunnell manufactured the chairs in a shop behind his home for about twenty-five years.[44] A rustic version of the chair is shown in figure 2-63.

Fig. 2-61. Adirondack settee, ca. 1894. Heart-and-star motif worked in mosaic twigwork; "Camp Uncas" spelled out on seat. (Photo: Courtesy of the Adirondack Museum, Blue Mountain Lake, New York)

Fig. 2-62. One of the original "Adirondack chairs," ca. 1914.
(Photo: Courtesy of the Adirondack Museum, Blue Mountain
Lake, New York)

Fig. 2-63.   A rustic version of the Adirondack chair.

A Recapitulation

At the time of the revival of rustic furniture in the 1830s and 1840s, the romantic movement, with all of its emphasis upon individual self-expression, the glorification of Nature and the simple life, and the return to genuine Christian ardor, was well established and even beginning to change course. By the 1830s, evidence of "the wholesale surrenders to the medieval mentality of contrition and subservience"[45] was visible throughout Europe and also in America. On both sides of the Atlantic, hairshirts were everywhere to be seen, hermits were in style, and the grotesque came out to watch the play. Strange, ascetic religious sects were formed in many regions of Europe. Quite a number of these immigrated to America, and the United States developed several varieties of its own. The celibate cabinetmakers of the Shakers earned a part of their livelihood by selling desexualized chairs. (They managed, however, to leave vestigial female breasts as knobs on the arms of the chairs and phallic acorns on the tops of the back posts.)

By and large, the nineteenth-century grotesque in America was buried so deeply beneath the layers of Victorian denial that it was rarely consciously acknowledged. P. T. Barnum's freaks, gory melodrama and folk paintings of murders, exhibited by traveling road shows, were relished for their direct cathartic value. There was, however, at least one place in nineteenth-century America where the observing function of the grotesque was alive and well—in the Appalachian Mountains.

Appalachian craftsmen tend to repeat, over and over, the traditional patterns of their cultural artifacts in a ritualistic identification with their past. We can see this attempt at repetition in the rustic chairs and settees of the second period. The "Spanish" bentwood chairs, however, were not a part of the mountain tradition. I have mentioned that the mountaineers enjoyed building the chairs, which is enough to classify them as folk art expression. Most people would agree that the seats produce a grotesque effect. Even odder is the slightly disconcerting impression upon the viewer that the chairs contain humor. There is also the suspicion (unwarranted) that the seats might not be structurally sound. The chairs exhibit a veritable delight in creating a riddle of their construction. It has been said that a riddle conceals what wit reveals.[46] The mountaineers were descended from a long line of authority-suspicious Celts, much given to concealing irreverent blasphemy beneath the cloaks of ambiguous riddles.

It is not until one attempts to copy these chairs that the humor can be appreciated. There is an enormous amount of tension in every piece of wood used in a chair, so much so that, until the final pieces have been nailed or locked into position, the chair will fly apart in all directions at the slightest touch.

If it were not for the fact that the mountaineers understood the nature of green wood perfectly, and had many opportunities to exploit its potential for tension in building animal traps, locks, fences, and the like, we might conclude that the craftsmen were simply testing out their control over Nature.

At the time in the late nineteenth century when these seats were being constructed, however, the outside world was beginning to impinge upon the freedom of the mountaineers in a very real way. In 1877, open warfare broke out between the distillers of moonshine and the federal collectors of whiskey excise taxes. In addition, "outlandish" summer tourists were crawling all over the mountains (some of them stumbling onto well-hidden stills). At the same time that they were constructing these chairs to sell to the tourists the mountaineers were conducting a private, but quite deadly civil war with the outlanders. I suspect that Rusticus, the chairmaker, was building a convoluted, tension-filled joke at the expense of Urbanus, the meddlesome, reform-minded Nature lover. There is an old Smoky Mountain story that is still a favorite in the mountains: A mother rushes into her house from the cornfield and calls out to her son, "Charlie, yonder comes some *tourists* up the holler! Git the pigs around to the front yard quick, so's they won't stop to talk!"

Beginning in the 1850s in England, the formal Italian garden was again creeping back into the picturesque landscape. By 1889, full topiary gardens had returned. Rustic bridges, benches, and summerhouses appeared. To some extent, rustic work in the Edwardian era took on the character of a dead metaphor. The revival had something of the character of a charmingly old-fashioned reminder of the distant eighteenth century. Rustic wood was a practical material for garden furniture and Edwardian designers managed to build some rather attractive pieces. The grotesque metaphor was not entirely dead, however; it simply moved over to the style known as art nouveau. Art nouveau is the lineal descendant of the Roman arabesques, in style and in content. We recall Vitruvius' fulminations: " . . . many little flower stalks unroll out of their roots and figures perch atop them, senselessly. Sometimes the stalks support half-length human figures. . . Such things, however, do not exist; they have never existed, nor shall they ever exist." On the contrary, they shall probably always exist.

The history of late twentieth-century rustic furniture remains to be written. An interesting paradox exists for future generations of our seemingly finite planet. If the worldwide shortage of timber occurs, as expected, by the year 2000, long-buried tree roots might become as valuable as polished mahogany. We shall then be forced, for the expression of grotesque taste, to return to irregular stone—and to ragout of lizard.

Oh the Roast Beef of *Old England,*
And *Old English* Roast Beef.

Rustic Summer House

PART II

Making Rustic Furniture

A grotesque rustic summerhouse in Burlingame, California, from a postal card, ca. 1909.

CHAPTER 3

The Technology

Rustic furniture is extremely easy to build. Depending upon the degree of refinement in design, it is well within the capacity of the veriest beginner. It cannot be emphasized too often that one of the greatest charms of rustic work lies in its irregularity and in the lack of mathematical precision in its construction. Unlike finished furniture, which demands meticulous measurements and careful joinery, rustic work is *enhanced* by an indifferent attitude toward the measuring stick. In most cases a chairmaker should build a rustic seat with but a few casual measurements and a greater reliance on the eye. Some respect is due the laws of gravity, to be sure, but far more attention should be given to the quality, configuration, and seasoning of the wood. In Chapter 6 will be found patterns for a number of pieces of rustic furniture. They are given as a guide for the beginning builder only. The real pleasure in making this furniture is to be found in learning to improvise with natural materials and an imaginative idea. To that end, Chapter 8 has been compiled to offer miscellaneous design ideas to start the imagination rolling.

If the craftsperson wishes to be free of bondage to the precision machine, man-made materials, and rigid rules of geometry, rustic furniture provides a golden opportunity. It is likely that the nineteenth century found rustic work attractive because of these features. The machines of the day could not reproduce the infinite variety of Nature's undulations between light and shade, no matter how much twinkling ornament designers applied to the furniture.

Despite the simplicity of its construction, rustic work uses a technology that has almost disappeared from the contemporary world. The modern woodworker knows little about his machine-sawn, standardized, mill-planed material as a growing tree—nor does he entirely need to. If he learns to use a lathe, he might ponder a moment about natural grain lines, but sandpaper will usually dispel his anxiety. Unless he attempts to copy a Windsor chair, he is free to cut, glue, and clamp away without ever needing to understand the incredible engineering of a standing tree. It is little noted outside the timber industry itself that it is the mass of opposing stress lines within the growing tree that enables the plant to stand upright.

Cleft wood, split apart with wedges rather than sawn, is rarely used by anyone today except wood sculptors and the manufacturers of baseball bats. Because it is split along the tree's natural cleavage lines, which are perpendicular to the growth rings, and not cut across the upright grain of the tree, cleft wood is stronger than sawn wood. The same is true of whole saplings.

Since rustic furniture makes use of small trees and limbs, the craftsperson will have to learn a new set of woodworking rules. The reward of this mastery is a magnificent surprise: The chairmaker learns to cooperate with his material, and in so doing develops a new way of perceiving and organizing design. The search for interesting forms and existing shapes in limbs, twigs, and roots has built-in rewards that are different from those of conventional cabinetmaking. One also learns to wait—for the tree's sap to go up or down, for limbs to grow to a bend, for the wood to dry.

Wood

The choice of wood depends upon the style of chair and whether it is to be used indoors or out. Apple, pear, and yew were the traditional woods used in the eighteenth century, according to Robert Manwaring. Rhododendron and laurel are highly durable and easy to work, but access to the wood is limited for most people. Hickory is probably the best all-around wood. It is very flexible while it is green; it has great strength and a good bark that will survive considerable weathering. White oak and ash have bending properties that are similar to hickory. Splints for weaving seats and backs can be taken from these last three woods. Red oak, birch, swamp dogwood, and some conifers are fairly durable out of doors, but beech, poplar, and maple are best used indoors. Walnut is perhaps too valuable to cut for rustic work. Locust, cedar, and cypress will withstand wet conditions, but they are not suitable for bending. Chestnut, alas, can no longer be considered; the greater pity because its capacity to survive weathering is legendary. Elm, a tree whose wood is flexible and whose limb configurations are quite often interesting, is impossible to cleave; furthermore, it will rot quickly if it is subjected to alternately wet and dry conditions.

All hardwoods and some softwoods may be used for indoor furniture. So long as the wood has a solid pith and tensile strength, it will serve. Because of its lightness, willow requires sturdy bracing. In fact, foundation frames of willow chairs are often made of stronger hardwoods.

It is a mistake to ascribe to willow a strength and character it does not possess. It is a wonderfully durable material when it is woven into basketwork chairs, but it probably should not be used with some of the spare styles of traditional rustic furniture made of harder woods. It may, however, be used as a supplement to other hardwoods—woven into splats or seats, or used for curved armrests. One may use small willow poles wherever it is possible to brace them securely. Certain varieties of swamp dogwood, hazel, and the shrublike red maple are very similar to willow in their bending properties, and these woods are much stronger, although not more durable out of doors.

Fretwork panels and small twigs for bracing or for decoration are taken ideally from fruit tree prunings, holly, boxwood, and, in fact, from an endless variety of hardwood twigs and tree roots found growing everywhere.

City dwellers are advised to cultivate a friendship with local tree surgeons and park departments. A saw, a hardhat, and a pile of freshly cut tree limbs will provide the urban craftperson with everything necessary for acquiring materials, although the pleasure of studying the configurations of limbs of standing trees and mentally designing a chair before cutting the wood is, of course, lost. Most tree surgeons are happy to give away branches and twigs provided the petitioner will work quickly, clean up the work area, and, above all, stay out of their way. It goes without saying that the wood must be cut from healthy branches.

It is customary to leave the bark on woods to be used out of doors, and it is this that dictates much of the special technology of the furniture. If the poles are to be stripped of bark, the wood can simply be seasoned, steamed, and bent in much the same way as one does with sawn wood, but the necessity of preserving the bark requires a different procedure.

Cutting and Seasoning

Rustic furniture is commonly made from sapling poles or from tree limbs, usually one to four inches [2.5–10cm] in diameter. Most of the difficulty encountered with rustic furniture lies with the proper seasoning of the poles. Some seats are made of green wood; some are made with partially seasoned upright posts and seasoned rungs; still others are made with fully seasoned wood.

The wood for making furniture to be used outdoors is cut in midwinter, when the sap is completely down. This is the only way to retain the bark. Tree bark is elastic, but not so much as is the sapwood lying just beneath it. If the tree is cut while its tissues are swollen with moisture, the wood will rapidly shrink away from the bark during the drying process.

Essentially, a tree is a set of hollow tubes and spongelike storage cells arranged in a conical form. All of this elaborately reticulated hollow system running throughout the tree enables the elastic wood, even when dry, to contract and expand in a never-ending effort to maintain a state of equilibrium with the humidity of its surroundings. The seasoning of wood concerns itself with one major task: The drying process must be so controlled that air will fill the honeycombed tubes and cells.[1] If a vacuum should form before air can reach the cell, the cell will eventually implode, and cracking and splitting of the wood will be inevitable.

As soon as the wood is cut, stand the butts of the poles in tin cans containing the wood preservative pentachlorophenol for about twelve hours. (Any bending of the wood, to be discussed later, is done at this time.) The poles should be propped upright against some support for air drying, under cover of a roof if possible. In this upright position, the wood will "bleed" a great deal of moisture from its hollow tubes. To discourage insects, slosh the pentachlorophenol all over the bark with a paintbrush and protect the butts from direct contact with the earth.

Total seasoning time depends upon the species of wood, the moisture content of the outside atmosphere, the amount of wind, and other influences of that sort. Complete open-air seasoning for a five-foot [1.5m] white oak pole with a three-inch [7.6cm] diameter can take from eleven months to three years. The process can, of course, be hurried along in a kiln, but the point I wish to make here is that open-air seasoning is a complex process and the only way to tell that optimum seasoning has been achieved is through experience gained from actually working with the woods. One learns to recognize the sound of dry wood and the feel of the weight of a sapling. There are no absolute standards established with respect to time. Unless a wood moisture meter is used, the worker will have to rely upon the development of some experience.

Proper and complete seasoning is a critical matter, especially if the furniture is to be used indoors. The humidity of the wood must not be much different from that of the air in which the finished piece will stand. If it is, shrinkage and cracking are real dangers as the wood expands or contracts in an effort to achieve equilibrium with the room's moisture level. This is, of course, a generalization; some woods can tolerate humidity differentials better than others. In general, major shrinkage occurs between 20-percent and 10-percent humidity. Depending on the region, the lowest moisture level that can be expected with air-drying—even with a dry, hot summer—is around 20 percent; yet the air in heated rooms in the winter frequently is as low as 10 percent. The result will be that the joints of the piece will become loose and some cracking will be evident.

Because it is not always possible to store air-dried wood in a heated indoor room to complete the seasoning process before the furniture is constructed, furniture makers may have to resort to an old trick; to wit: using partially seasoned uprights and fully dry rungs. In this way, the joints will become firmly locked as the green posts shrink around the ends of the tenoned dry rungs. The traditional practice in the Appalachians was to season the rungs for a few weeks outside and then to complete the drying by standing them in front of a fireplace or an indoor stove. The rungs would usually dry within a month. Nails are unnecessary if this technique is used.

If the furniture is to be used exclusively out of doors, the wood can be worked in the autumn following the winter cutting season. In this case, the joints are usually tenoned and nails are added to insure tightness.

Willow furniture is more or less "thrown together" while the rods and poles are still green—chiefly, to save the time involved in bending and drying the rods in a frame. Inevitably, willow furniture constructed in this fashion will shrink and pull away from the nails that must be used to secure the rods. After one or two seasons of drying, the chairs become loose and wobbly. Often, they can be renailed, but they remain rather fragile.

Bending

If moist heat is applied to a seasoned pole (the common method employed in bending wood), the bark will promptly peel off. This is why the wood used for rustic work must be bent when it is green.

Many chairmakers in the Appalachians used the ingeniously simple method of bending *growing* saplings in the early spring when their rising sap made them most pliable. The curves were bent and tied with ropes and allowed to grow under tension until the following winter, when they were cut. This is, by far, the easiest method to use. Other methods of bending require the use of a bending brake and some simple tension devices.

Chairmakers also took advantage of the appearance of natural curves and interesting growth distortions when they could find them. Small saplings growing underneath larger trees at the edges of cleared land frequently bend themselves in interesting ways to reach light. Additionally, certain vines grow in a natural helix and will imprint a spiral pattern on a young sapling on which they grow. (See fig. 2-20, page 50.)

If the chairmaker can find a slender sapling that is heavily branched, it will be possible to trim the twigs from the outside of the pole, to bend the entire pole into shape for the chair back, and then to weave the twigs growing from the inside of the sapling into a splat. The ends of the twigs emerging from the weaving are trimmed to fit flat against the inside of the posts and then nailed with small brads to the upright stiles. The twigs should not be much larger than a pencil. Larger twigs, growing laterally, make it very hard to bend the main bow of the back because of the knotholes, which will extend all the way to the heartwood of the sapling. Fruit trees are quite suitable for the technique.

The roots of a number of hardwood trees and shrubs are unusually malleable. It is backbreaking labor to uncover tree roots carefully, but trees growing on sandy-soiled riverbanks are not too difficult to dig out.

Begin digging with a mattock about twelve feet [3.6m] away from the trunk of a large tree. Gently expose one or two lateral roots of the diameter desired for the framework; then, using small garden tools, remove the soil very gently from the roots, taking care not to sever the rootlets from the main stem. Try to determine which side of the major root will serve as the inside of the chair back as soon as it is possible to see enough of the root system. In this way, the rootlets growing from the other sides can simply be cut off with the mattock. The longer the pencil-sized rootlets, the easier it will be to weave the splat. After clearing the earth from the long roots, chop the segment you have chosen from the main root and dig it out.

Bend the piece into shape while it is still wet. Tie the ends of the posts to secure the shape of the bend and then weave the rootlets into a splat. Carefully trim any extraneous rootlets from the rest of the frame, rinse dirt and mud from the wood with a garden hose, and set aside the chair back to season.

If there happens to be a woodworker anywhere in Western civilization with enough determination and patience to make the ultimate in rustic work, I will just add that it is perfectly possible to prune the limbs of a young apple or pear tree over a period of about three years to create a growth pattern that will be suitable for making this all-in-one kind of chair back. Appalachian canemakers used to create interesting forms for the shafts and the bent handles of the canes by training apple branches to shape. Fruit trees are particularly adaptable to this treatment. The twigs can be twisted, tied in knots, and even grafted together with the techniques commonly employed in espalier work.

If a sapling is to be bent to a curve with a short radius, such as would be required for a bow back or a curved armrest, some type of bending frame will be required. A smooth, flowing curve can rarely be formed without one. Steamed, seasoned wood is bent with a continuous, fairly rapid motion; green wood, on the other hand, is bent in stages to allow the fibers time to stretch. The compression on the underside of the curve will have to work its way up through the tension of the fibers on the convex side of the curve. Both heat and moisture facilitate this rather traumatic rearrangement of the internal stresses in wood, but, again, the problem of the bark intrudes.

Canemakers in England used to bend seasoned limbs with the bark intact by heating the poles in damp sand. Theoretically, however, the bark will peel any time there is a swelling in the sapwood to which the bark cannot adjust itself. Where an old chair has been in contact with the earth, for example, the bark ringing the lower legs will often have peeled. (If poles are inverted on the legs of the chair, this will be less of a problem, since water is drawn *upward* from the butts of trees by capillary action.)

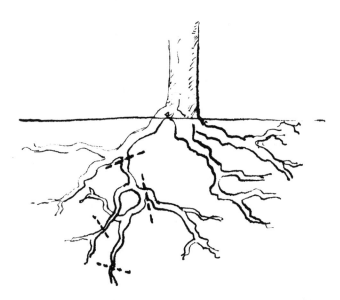

Fig. 3-1.

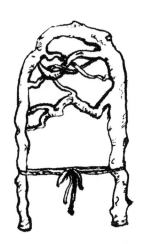

Fig. 3-2.

Bending Frames

There are several simple devices that can be used to form a curve with green wood. If the pole is no larger than one inch [2.5cm] in diameter, the device shown in figure 3-3 can be used. The curve is first started by making slight bends along the entire length of the pole either by bracing it with a foot while bending by hand (fig. 3-4a) or by pulling or pushing the sapling against a standing tree trunk (fig. 3-4b). If the pole will not bend easily, this method will have to be given up in favor of the wooden frame in figure 3-7. Once the initial bends have been made, the pole is lashed firmly to the simple frame and allowed to season for a few days, or long enough for the "memory" of the curve to be set in the wood. There may be some recovery when the pole is removed, but if it can be pushed back into the curved shape easily the bending task will have been accomplished.

Bends with slight curves can be pulled into shape gradually with the use of the windlass arrangement shown in figure 3-5. These mild bends will need to season under tension for at least three weeks. When the compression on the concave side and the tension on the convex side of a curve are nearly equal in force, the wood will be more likely to spring back to its former straight position. The pole will have to be held under tension until some seasoning occurs. Poles with slight curves should always be overbent; they will spring back a bit under the best of circumstances.

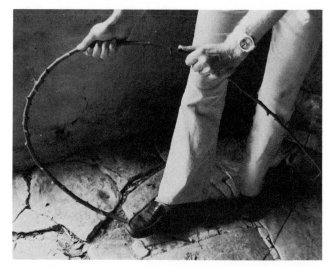

Fig. 3-4a.

Fig. 3-4b.

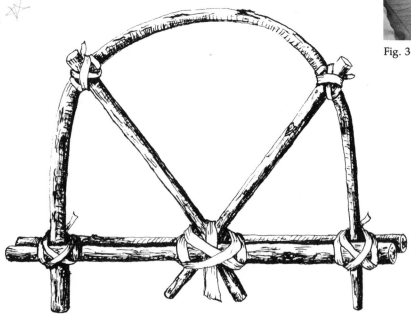

Fig. 3-3.

82

Growing saplings should be bent in early spring. Thick saplings, two inches [5cm] or more in diameter, are bent over a period of several days. The windlass method is used here, too; however, two or three lateral struts of graduated lengths will be needed to produce a flowing curve (fig. 3-6). Without the struts, the sapling will bend at the apex of the curve and something resembling a Gothic arch will result.

To make this sort of bend, first loop over the trunk and the pulled-down top of the sapling a rope with a small pulley (or a metal ring) attached to one end. Tighten the free end of the rope slowly—pulling at short intervals—until the longest strut can be positioned; then tie the windlass rope in place and tighten it with a stick. Remove the pulley rope and allow the tree to adjust itself for a day or two. At the next tightening session, loosen the windlass, replace the strut with a shorter one, and retighten the windlass. The process is repeated every few days until the bow can be drawn into the desired radius. Some trees can be bent in a single session; others might take several sessions. The tree is not cut until the following winter.

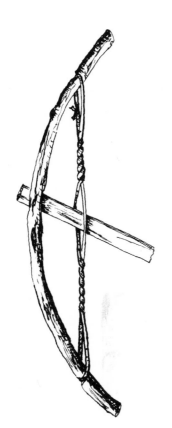

Fig. 3-5.

Fig. 3-6.

Bending on a Solid Frame

Any number of irregular shapes can be formed with the use of a specially made bending table. (Fig. 3-7) The technique described is for making a bow-shaped back.

Construct a template of glued up stock two inches [5cm] thick. This is cut out on a band saw and attached to a larger block of wood, either with metal bolts or with nails. Drill a number of peg holes in the bottom block around the perimeter of the template and about two inches [5cm] from the edge of the template. Add other peg holes from one to two inches [2.5–5cm] out from the first set. Cut tapered square pegs to fit the holes and, at the same time, make several small wedges.

Clamp the frame to a waist-high table. Place the center of the pole to be bent between the template and a tight peg at the top of the bow. Drive a wedge between the peg and the pole, taking care not to scar the bark. (A scrap piece of heavy leather placed against the bark will protect it.)

Working on alternate sides, pull the pole gradually into position around the template and peg it. If the pole is resistant, set the pegs into the outer row of holes until about two-thirds of the bend has been completed; then return to the top and work the pole closer to the frame. Allow a brief pause between each bending movement to permit the stress of the compression to distribute itself through the length of the wood. If there are gaps between the pole and the template, insert wedges between the pegs and the pole. Allow the pole to set to shape overnight. Tie ends with a rope, remove pegs, and set the piece aside to season for a week. Always allow a margin of two to three inches [5–7.6cm] at the ends of any pole to be bent. The ends can be trimmed to size when the chair is made.

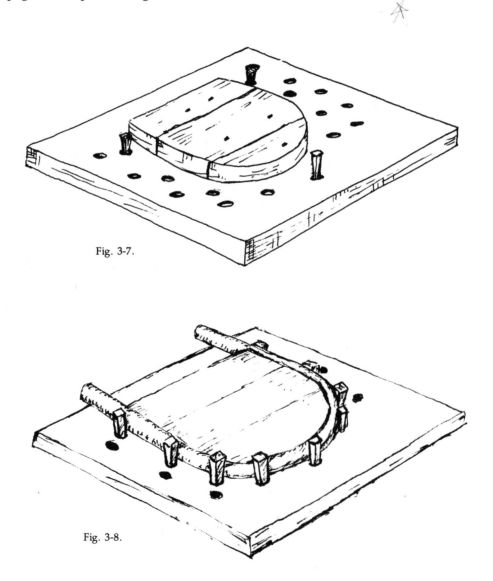

Fig. 3-7.

Fig. 3-8.

Single Bends in Straight Poles

Posts for legs are usually splayed by means of single bends at the level of the seat rails. The green poles are bent with leverage in a brake. The limbs of a forked tree can be used for this leverage; a better method, however, is to drive a couple of large iron spikes into an upright post or a large standing tree. (Fig. 3-9) Leather or rubber sleeves placed over the spikes will protect the bark of the pole. The pole is placed between the spikes and overbent slightly with firm downward pressure applied on one end.

If the wood will not retain the bend, it will have to season while tied to an angled block of seasoned hardwood. (Fig. 3-10) The block can be made from a two-foot [61cm] length of 2″ × 5″ [5 × 12.7cm] stock. Cut the desired angle on the top of the block and notch the lower edge in order to keep the ropes or leather straps from slipping.

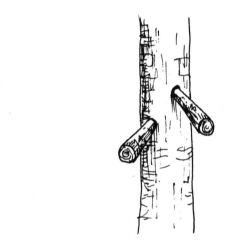

Fig. 3-9.

Fig. 3-10.

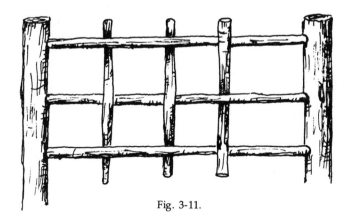

Fig. 3-11.

Another way to season these bent uprights is to weave them between the rungs of a sturdy fence. (Fig. 3-11) Use a wedge of wood between the pole and the top rail if necessary to maintain the proper angle of the bend.

Measurement

The taper and the irregularity of natural materials preclude the building of a matched pair of rustic seats. After building one or two pieces of the furniture, the craftsperson will probably find that the first tool to be discarded is the calibrated ruler; it simply gets in the way of the progress of the construction, especially if the chair is being designed as the work goes along.

It is easier to use notched stick gauges and knotted diagonal strings or flat sticks; the use of simple geometry will be a far more practical method of measurement than the tedious reliance upon the carpenter's rule. Where sections of poles are to be of identical length, the craftsperson can measure, or estimate, the length of the first one and then use this piece as a guide for cutting all others. A simple way to locate 90-degree angles around circular posts to be drilled for mortises is to wrap a strip of thin paper around the post, mark off the circumference, and then to fold the paper into quarters; the 90-degree points will be located at the creases. A plumb bob and a spirit level are useful occasionally, and these devices save time and energy, too.

I am not advocating careless craftsmanship—far from it—but we have become so accustomed to the standards of narrow tolerances dictated by the use of machine tools that we have forgotten the charm and even the creative humanity in the slight unevenness of handwork. Machines *are* only tools, and boring ones at that, when we use them to the exclusion of our human right to inspired eccentricity. Rustic furniture that bears the marks of undue concern with its construction is a failure. In its fundamental expression it exists as a demonstrable symbol of the relaxation of the stringencies of decorum and all that "up-tight" Academic art stands for. Mathias Darly's chairs were designed for *fun*.

Joinery

Although rustic furniture will be more durable if its parts are joined by mortise-and-tenon joints, typically it is joined with only simple butt joints. A sharp chisel is used to square a ledgelike slot in a round pole to receive the sawn end of a horizontal rail. (Fig. 3-12) Nail holes are predrilled and the nails driven in. In green hardwoods, select a drill bit with a diameter larger than ordinarily would be used for seasoned wood; otherwise, the wood will split as it shrinks around the nails. Several simple joints for nailing are shown in figures 3-13 through 3-16.

Figure 3-16 illustrates a method of joining parts with hardwood dowels. The dowels should be seven-eighths of an inch [2.2cm] in diameter for two-inch [5cm] stock. The joining member is scribed and cut to fit against a circular post.

Mortise and tenon joints (figs. 3-17 and 3-18), as we have mentioned, provide the most secure construction in chairs. Mortise holes are drilled in the vertical posts with a brace and an expandable bit.

(Spoon bits can be used, but since the end of a spoon bit has a tendency to wander off course, drill a pilot hole first.) Make V-cut cradles from blocks of wood to keep the round poles from rolling, or wedge the poles securely against a stop with wooden wedges. For the tenon, score the same circle on the end of the rung with a compass or with the spur of the expandable bit itself. Pare the stock from the tenon with a penknife or clamp the rung in a vise and shave the tenon with a drawknife. Tenons may be cut on a lathe, or they may be trimmed with an old-fashioned circular plane called a *witchet*. A witchet works rather like a pencil sharpener. It is desirable to pare the stock next to the tenon slightly to create a shoulder. Mortises are usually from one-half to three-quarters of an inch [1.3–1.9cm] in diameter.

If you are tenoning a seasoned rung into green-wood, shave about one-sixteenth of an inch [.16cm] from both sides of the tenon. Because wood shrinks across the grain, a circular post becomes slightly ovoid when seasoned. Shaving the tenon will prevent the post's splitting as it dries around the end of the rung.

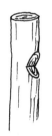

Fig. 3-13.

Fig. 3-14.

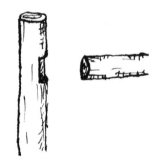

Fig. 3-12.

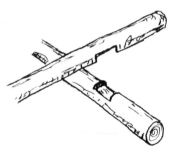

Fig. 3-15.

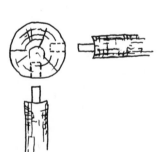

Fig. 3-16.

Fig. 3-17.

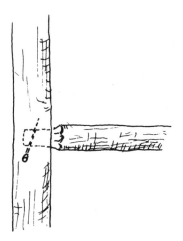

Fig. 3-18.

Fig. 3-19. Shaving the end of a tenon with a drawknife.

Nails

On willow and slender hardwood rods, use thin box nails ranging in size from 8d to three-quarter-inch [1.9cm] wire brads. Nails should be just long enough to reach through the second nailing member. Should the end of a nail protrude, cut it off with wire cutters. Nails cannot be clinched successfully in green or soft woods. A small anvil or a block of hardwood is useful for nailing hard-to-reach parts. Maneuver the chair frame over the anvil until it provides a backing to hammer against.

Larger sized common and finishing nails, or wood screws, may be used at times. Visible screw heads should be countersunk and concealed by gluing sawdust or a patch of bark over the hole.

Sighting Angles

The major difference between a cabinetmaker and a chairmaker is that the cabinetmaker thinks in terms of the boundaries of linear measurement, the hypotenuse of angles, whereas the chairmaker visualizes the three-dimensional space within (and without) the various angles in a chair. This is probably why chairmakers become skilled at estimating diagonal lines. It is a skill that develops quickly with practice, and it is a technique that will sharpen any craftsperson's sense of spatial design. The use of simple, often imaginary geometry to locate centers, angles, and boundary outlines is extremely helpful in building chairs. A chairmaker designs a chair from the inside out, not the outside in. Space is not enclosed by a chair, it is carved up by the object; consequently, the chairmaker must learn to regard negative space, the air in and around the positive lines of the chair.

No doubt, the novice will prefer to use a bevel square or a jig to drill mortises, but soon enough he will discover that drilling them by sight is not all that difficult. The major obstacle is gathering the courage to try it. The procedure is as follows: With the height of the hole already marked on the post, position the drill bit on the line in the center of the post. Lean back a foot or so to study the angles formed by the post and the bit. Move around to get the feel of several positions. Imagine the entire framework of the chair, using the post as the point of orientation. Try to *feel* the shape of the angle. When the angled position of the bit seems right, extend some imaginary lines beyond the outlines of the chair and use these extensions to visualize the reciprocal angles. This is a most useful check on the original estimation. One usually experiences a sudden awareness of the correctness of the angle, so much so that the hole, and the depth of it, can be drilled with utter confidence. Some people find it easier to acquire the knack of sighting angles if the posts are clamped in a vertical position. A drill press remains for the overly timid.

Root Chairs and Naturalistic Furniture

The undercarriage of a chair must be engineered in such a way that it will support weight and remain stable; in the case of natural wood, this usually means that the chair will have to have some straight length sections in the legs to provide strength. Small gnarled roots, made up of irregular curves, will give way under weight. The straight legs can be disguised by wrapping roots around them in an irregular way or by drawing attention away from the legs through ornamental elaboration elsewhere in the chair.

One of the most difficult tasks in making this kind of grotesque furniture is to simulate natural growth. The idea is to make the seat look as if it were a still-growing mass of woody tree roots, freshly plucked from the dark, elemental forest. The chair should be asymmetrical and full of knobs and bulges, wildly irregular, and yet it should be comfortable to sit in. If possible, weave the roots into the fabric of the chair, concealing cut ends on the inside of the frame. In figure 1-3 (page 21), note the "drop-in," or inset, seat. Such a seat is most appropriate to this type of chair because it seems to be an integral part of the structure.

Occasionally, the lines of an original chair or settee or a table base will seem to leap from the gnarled branches of a tree. Try to see the form within the branch. A chair requires an undercarriage of some sort (to lift the seat from the ground), a seat, a back support, and, if desired, arm supports. With these requirements in mind, search out likely components for a comfortable chair contained within the configuration of the tree limbs. For example, in the limbs of the tree in figure 3-20 may be found one entire side of a settee, missing only a front leg. The matching side of the settee may well be found in a tree of the same species growing nearby, or one might locate a matching side with a *back* leg missing—there is no rule that says rustic furniture has to be symmetrical. The intent is to provide a comfortable, stable piece with an ingenious, thrifty use of the materials. During my travels in the Virginia mountains, I encountered a rustic baby crib whose top rails had been almost completely debarked by young human teeth. While I was examining the piece (and thinking privately that rustic cribs are potentially dangerous to teething babies), I was startled to catch a very faint scent of wintergreen. The rails of the crib had been made with sweet birch (*Betula lenta*), the material of the original mountain toothbrush—naturally flavored with wintergreen.

One of the charms of settees built around tree trunks, or attached to the trees, is that the entire tree can be used for shelter and for seating with a minimum of material and effort.

Beds

Bed frames, built to support the weight of modern box springs and mattresses, present a problem regarding scale. The bed rails should have a thickness of at least four inches [10.2cm] to keep them from sagging. The bulk of a four-inch round pole, however, may be overpowering in a small bedroom. For this reason, it is probably better to use a metal frame for springs and mattress and to confine the rustic decoration to the headboard or to a tall box frame constructed from finer material. Such frames can be quite inventive. Wild grapevines, in particular, are useful materials for the decoration of canopied bed frames. (Grapevines, incidentally, will not survive long in furniture used outdoors.) Soak grapevines in a pond for about a week to render them pliable.

Fig. 3-20.

Tabletops

Rustic tabletops always present something of a style problem. To be practical, a tabletop should be smooth, but such a large area of planed wood in a piece of rustic furniture is discordantly out of place. The flat plane requires some random shadow in it to break up the reflected light. Short of veneering a flat tabletop with wide strips of rough bark, some compromise will have to be made.

Three methods were employed in the past. First, a number of straight rods were nailed onto supporting cleats, making a "corduroy" top suitable for holding lamps, books, and the like, but too irregular for glasses of liquid. (See fig. 6-4.) Second, a regular top was made of planed wood, joined with dowels and glue, and then an apron of split half-round twigs was nailed around the perimeter (fig. 2-50), or, third, an overall mosaic pattern, sometimes called Swiss work, was formed by nailing split half-round twigs over a geometric pattern drawn on a smooth wooden base (figs. 2-25 and 2-61).

The best-looking tops, especially for large tables, and perhaps the easiest to construct can be made by nailing short, random-length, tongue-in-groove hardwood flooring strips to a piece of one-inch [2.5 cm] plywood. (The narrow-width oak strips look best, because of the scale, but they are difficult to locate.) Bevel the top edge of the completed tabletop and glue and nail pieces of half-round twigs to the side edges, or use beveled flooring strips for the edging; then use a dark stain and varnish the top with a dull varnish.

Other methods include veneering a plywood top with pieces of rawhide leather. And, finally, turning a group of children loose on a planed top with a wood-burning iron and some small carving tools is guaranteed to add rustic shadows and priceless personality to any tabletop. Adolescents, in particular, have a natural aptitude for grotesque graffiti.

CHAPTER 4

Design

Types of Rustic Furniture

There are at least three approaches to rustic furniture. The first is simply to construct a well-designed piece of useful garden furniture, using natural materials, usually with the bark intact to preserve the wood from weathering. This method is simple, inexpensive, and practical. Design principles for such furniture follow those used for construction in finished wood, except that the scale of the material used out of doors can be much larger because the "rooms" are larger.

The second type of furniture makes use of basketry techniques, or basketry combined with traditional methods of wood joinery. In these objects, small, flexible elements are interlaced, twined, looped, in such a way that the counterforces within the materials tend to lock the pieces together. This approach exploits the natural structural tendencies of the material. An easy way to create a design for a rustic seat of this type is to make up a number of miniature chairs using damp quarter-inch (.64cm) rattan reed or slender green willow rods or some other flexible twigs. Lines of support for the frames will suggest themselves as the little chairs are developed.

A third type of rustic furniture expresses the comic and the fearful grotesque. It can range from satirical travesties of well-known styles of furniture, through Walt Disney-like anthropomorphic tree forms, to hideous chaos, from a clever play on man-made form to an indistinct mass of distorted natural forms. It is impossible for one person to tell another *how* to play, but I can say at least that play upon mental contrasts is the essence of this kind of furniture.

Since all three types of rustic furniture depend for their success upon some statement of organized design as a foil for contrast, I shall list here a few principles of design organization. Not surprisingly, many of them are gifts borne from the Greeks. Among their many refined and glorious accomplishments, the Greeks developed a formidable understanding of the laws of optics and human perception. In contrast to the later Academies, however, they were never afraid to break these rules of design when it served their artistic purposes.

Rustic furniture is particularly suited to the so-called barbarian Gothic style, but beyond pointing out that multiplicity of forms, irregularity of linear outline, and surprise characterize the Gothic, no one has ever succeeded in defining its limits, primarily because it is an art of infinite natural form, variety, and imaginative improvisation. Novelty and sensation alone are short-lived effects. The Gothic succeeds in sustaining sensation by multiplying complex parts.

Most likely, the designer of rustic furniture will tend to employ both the Greek and Gothic styles. Be warned, however, that a real pitfall awaits the one who tries to make a silk purse out of a sow's ear. As Edmund Burke pointed out in the eighteenth century, the picturesque is rough, the beautiful is smooth; hence the problem with tabletops. Rustic furniture does not belong to the category of the beautiful. The grotesque may be clever and sophisticated, but the source of its energy belongs to a less mature stage of our mental and emotional life than does the beautiful.

Design Principles

Good design in a three-dimensional object is a complicated matter of assembling structural elements in such a way that the object serves its function with an economical and practical use of the material of which it is constructed, that the space in the object is pleasingly divided horizontally and vertically, that any ornamentation in or upon the object is in harmony with the design and fitting to the use of the object, and that a good proportion is maintained both in the two-dimensional planes of the object and in the relationship among all of the several units of the object's mass.[1]

Function

The first and most obvious feature in the design of chairs is that they have severe limits. In order to serve as comfortable seats, their design must conform to the limitations of the structure of the human body: The seat height can rarely be more than eighteen inches [46cm] (sixteen inches [41cm] is better for outdoor use); chair arms have to be about seven or eight inches [17.8–20cm] higher than the seat; and the major support angles in the chair are fixed within a rather narrow range of degrees.

Because a chair must conform to the body, the designer begins with a lesson in anatomy. Figure 4-1 shows a figure seated in a chair that will produce a state of tension in the muscles because the head is off balance and the back is unsupported. In addition, discomfort will result at the pressure points on the pelvic bone and on the thigh.[2]

Figure 4-2 shows the body posture in a state of relaxation, with the body weight balanced and supported by the structure of the chair. Rustic furniture is, by its nature, intended to be used for informal relaxation. Human dignity, usually indicated by an upright, muscularly controlled posture, is not under consideration here; therefore, a chair that will allow a comfortably relaxed, even slouching posture is acceptable. By drawing on scaled graph paper stick figures seated in chairs, the chairmaker can measure angles with a protractor and simply apply the measurements to the wood.

Division of Horizontal and Vertical Planes

Although it is true that a chair is a three-dimensional object, it is singular in that the structural pieces of the chair—seat rails, rungs, stretchers, backs—make up nearly all the divisions and subdivisions of space on the *two-dimensional* plane.

It is an old rule of esthetics that a flat plane is more pleasing if it is either definitely vertical or definitely horizontal—in other words, some form of a rectangle. Round or square shapes do not meet this qualification and, therefore, frequently lack interest.

The dominant lines, moreover, on either a vertical or a horizontal plane should lead the eye in the dominant direction. When a vertical plane is to be divided into two or more parts, for example, the best effect is achieved by making the divisions unequal in size. In a chair, this often occurs naturally, the chair back usually being higher than the distance from floor to seat. If a vertical rectangle is divided into three parts,

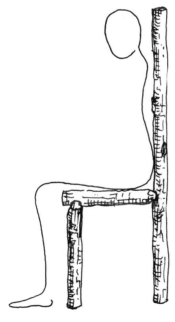

Fig. 4-1.

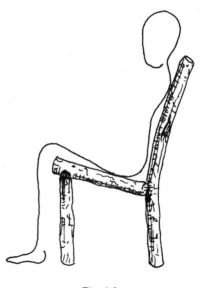

Fig. 4-2.

one of the areas should dominate the others; the dominant area may be placed either between two unequal rectangular areas or at the bottom with the other areas stacked on top of it. Divisions of vertical planes should suggest stability of weight. Our sense of the laws of gravity should not be offended by the appearance of disproportionate weight distribution.

It is the need for a logical appearance of weight balance that underlies rules given for the division and subdivision of horizontal planes as well. Horizontal rectangles are most effectively divided by placing a large rectangle between two smaller ones of equal size. Alternately, a rectangle may be subdivided into two or several areas, all *alike* in size and shape but arranged in a symmetrical position.

Asymmetrical balance, difficult to achieve in chair design, can be used to good effect provided the bulk on one side of an imaginary fulcrum appears to balance an unequal area or bulk on the other side.

Curved Lines and Decoration

All of the rules just outlined apply to straight lines and flat planes. They might be useful in the design of rustic work made of straight length sections of saplings; we recall, however, Nature's abhorrence of straight lines.

Curves in rustic furniture are of two orders. First, there is the curve that the craftsperson creates from straight material in imitation of Nature's growth lines (and the rules given here pertain to these "idealized" curves). The second order involves the use of real curves in the natural growth of trees, the distortions and irregularities that result from "accidents" in the unrefined life of the growing tree.

Man-made curves have been abstracted and refined from the observation of Nature in order to ornament structural outline and to soften the transition between structure and ornament. For example, in the table in figure 2-50 (page 67), one can see that the superstructure is composed of a series of triangles; one can also see that the builder has softened this rigid structural geometry by adding two sets of helical lines, twisting in opposite directions.

Almost all of the rules regarding curves are based upon growth patterns in Nature. It is pleasing to see curves with rhythmical movement and geometrical variety. Nature's plants grow in the pattern of the helix and with logarithmic progression; hence the spiral and the volute. A compass curve is mechanical and boring because of the lack of variety in its arc, the sameness of its radii.

Pleasing curves have dominant and subordinate elements. A long, graceful, curving line (with no straight line whatever in it) should end in a quick terminal curve or a reverse curve, rather like the line formed by snapping a long slender willow rod

through the air. The movement of idealized curved lines in wood suggests the graceful swaying of tree limbs in a breeze. When the radius of a curve is shortened and the wave motion is crowded, we register the analogy to the motion of a tree in a storm. Curves should seem to unfold the way a new leaf unfolds from the bud.

It is generally believed that a curved line should have no abrupt change of direction in it; this, however, is where rustic furniture parts company with the Academy. Tree limbs and roots do have abrupt, jerky lines and these can be exploited with splendid rustic effect. Rustic curves do not have to be lyrical and slow moving or decorous.

The designer should know that a curve will create a sense of movement. It is the designer's choice where the movement will go and how much movement will be expressed. Furthermore, outline curves will compete with any curves used in surface decoration. Careful attention should be given to striking a balance between the two or they will cancel each other out. Note that curves in the framework of the doll's chair in figure 2-44 have been held to a gentle minimum in order to exhibit the back panel.

Proportion

Good proportion is the glue that unites disparate elements in a design. It is the result of a pleasing visual relationship between length and width in any given area of the several parts of an object, as well as the relationship of the parts to the whole mass of an object. A satisfying awareness of organization, unity, and harmony is produced in a three-dimensional object if all of the parts are related to one another in the same, or in a similar, proportion. (The numerical expression of proportion is obtained by dividing the length by the width. The ratio 3:5 means that the short side of a rectangle is composed of three parts of a given length and that the long side is made up of five parts of the same length.)

For all of its importance, the effect of good proportion is extremely subtle. In fact, the less obvious it is, the more pleasing. Simple ratios, such as 1:1 or 1:2, seem dull to us because they lack variety. The rectangle and the oval are more interesting than the square and the circle. It should be pointed out that extreme proportions, such as 1:20, are too complex to be perceived at all.

Chairs, as I have said, and many other pieces of furniture have certain size limitations because of their function. A practical way to design the space in a chair is to use the fixed limits (seat height, for example) as the measure from which all other proportions are derived. Make a scaled frontal drawing of the chair and compute the outlines of the chair using about three different proportions, such as 2:3, 3:5, or 5:8;

then select the most pleasing outline. Using the same proportion, compute the areas of the other horizontal and vertical subdivisions. Draw the side elevation of the chair and repeat the computations. Once the chair has been proportioned, the designer may proceed to play with different structural and decorative ideas, usually by placing a sheet of overlay paper over the original sketch.

It is not easy to maintain good proportions throughout the three-dimensional space (some of it imaginary) contained within the outlines of a solid geometric figure; one has to learn to visualize cubic space. If, however, an object has been unified from its very inception by a consistent hidden proportion, it remains endlessly satisfying and stimulating to our perception. A sense of logical order and the assurance of rhythmic interest is built into such an object. All other pleasing decorative details added to the object are simply frosting on a very good cake.

Finishes

Outdoor furniture will survive longer if it is protected with varnish or paint. Apply all finishes only after the wood has been well seasoned.

Varnish

If a darker color is desired, stain the furniture with an oil-based stain. Seal the wood with two coats of orange shellac, thinned with one part denatured alcohol to one part shellac. After the shellac has dried, apply two or three coats of spar varnish, thinned half and half with turpentine. Dull the final coat by rubbing the surface with 0000 steel wool. A glossy surface is inappropriate on rustic furniture.

Paint

Either a forest green or a dark brown color should be used; marine enamel is recommended because it weathers well. Seal the wood with a primer coat, then apply the marine enamel. Use thinned coats to avoid a heavy buildup of paint.

Rustic furniture should be removed to indoor storage during the winter months. The furniture will decay if it is not protected somewhat from weather. Do not allow chair legs to remain constantly in low-lying, poorly drained areas. Small pieces of slate may be used under the feet, but metal caps placed around the bottoms of the legs should be outlawed—not only are they unsightly, but they promote rot by sealing off the circulation of air.

CHAPTER 5

Seat Weaving

Seats and back panels for chairs can be woven of white oak, hickory, or ash splints; strips of smooth outer and inner barks of various trees; strips of leather; or wide strips of rattan cane. (See p. 121 for sources of supply.)

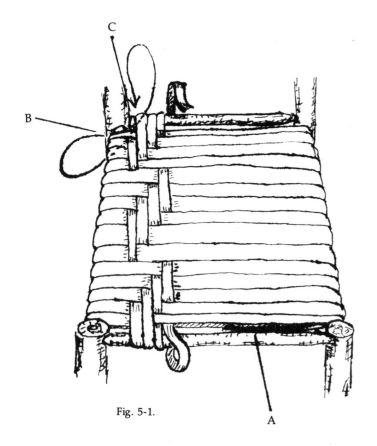

Fig. 5-1.

Beginning at point A in figure 5-1, tack the end of a well-dampened or a green splint to the inside of the front seat rail. Wrap the warp around the two side seat rails, covering the rails closely. Join new splints as needed on the underlayer of the warp by overlapping them about three inches [7.6cm] and stapling them together, or by tying the splints on notches with cord or wire. Complete the warping at point B, leaving at least a thirty-inch [76cm] length of splint. Take the end of the splint diagonally beneath the seat, to the inside of the rear post, and carry it up over the rear seat rail, as at point C. Weave, in the pattern you have chosen, at a right angle to the warp, straight to the front rail. Continue weaving across bottom layer of the warp; carry weaver up over the rear seat rail in preparation to weave row two. Filling in the weft continues until the rear seat rail has been completely covered. Cut off end of final weft splint and tack it under the rear seat rail. The weft will finish on the bottom side of the seat.

In most cases, the front seat rail is wider than the rear; therefore, two triangular areas of the seat will remain to be filled with weft after the central rectangle has been woven. Since the weft cannot be wrapped continuously around the back seat rail, the triangles will have to be pieced. Beginning on the top layer of the seat, near a back post, and keeping pattern regular, hook three or four inches [7.6–10.2cm] of a well-dampened splint over one of the warp splints and weave forward over the front rail and back across the bottom layer until the splint reaches close to the back post. Fold splint back over warp, as in figure 5-2; cut off the end and lodge it beneath the warp. Return to the top of the seat and fill in the remaining space, moving forward in a stepwise progression along the side seat rail until the front rail has been completely covered by the pieced weavers.

In weaving back panels, some care must be taken to prevent the joins from showing on the back of the panel. When weft splints have to be joined on the back, it is customary merely to overlap the ends through several warp splints (five or six inches [12.7–15.2cm]), concealing the two ends beneath the warp splints. After one or two rows of weaving have been worked, the join will be wedged snugly into place.

A twill pattern forms a closely woven texture well suited to chair seats. Do not use fancy weaving patterns for the seats and backs of rustic furniture, as a "busy" pattern will compete with the rustic appearance of the wood in the chair.

Weaving Patterns for Wide Binding Cane

An open-mesh weave is suitable for half-inch [1.3cm] wide rattan cane. The weave is strong and, because it permits air circulation, cool.

Use two strands of well-dampened cane. Tack them to the inside of frame at point A in figure 5-3. Keeping the strands parallel, wrap the warp around the frame, taking an extra turn around each side rung. The weft is attached to the frame and woven over and under the doubled warp strands, again taking the extra turn around the rod of the frame. (Fig. 5-4)

With wide cane, new strands are added by joining them at the stretcher rails or the seat rails. (Fig. 5-5) Since the two strands will run out at about the same time, the ends are staggered to permit one of them to be joined to a new end at one rail and the other end to be joined at the opposite rail. The old and the new ends are given a half twist, the new end is tucked back under the old wrapping and the old end is snugged against the rail and wrapped in with the binding as the weaving proceeds.

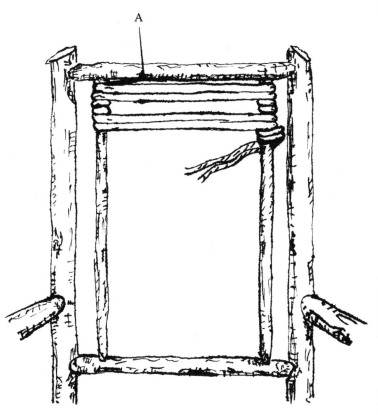

Fig. 5-3.

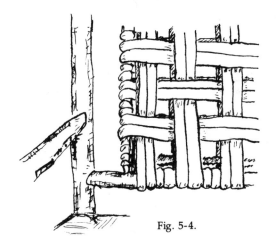

Fig. 5-4.

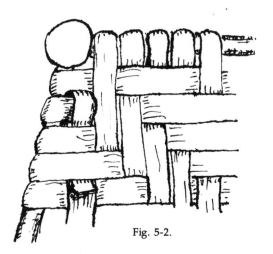

Fig. 5-2.

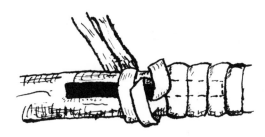

Fig. 5-5.

95

CHAPTER 6

Patterns

In this chapter will be found several recipes for rustic seats (and one table), arranged in order of difficulty. It is part of the contradictory nature of rustic furniture that exactitude with respect to the listed measurements of the material is highly approximate. The pieces can be made with or without a painful search through the forest for saplings of the precise diameters given in the patterns. Once you have grasped the technical essentials of working with green wood, or with round stock, the chances are that you will no longer be interested in following any pattern but your own, and that is just what the furniture is all about.

Child's Willow Chair

Precut

2 front leg posts	10″ × 1″ diameter	[25.4 × 2.5cm]
2 back leg posts	20″ × 1″	[50.8 × 2.5cm]
13 rails	15″ × 3/4″	[38 × 1.9cm]
8 arm rods	4′ × 1/2″	[1.2m × 1.3cm]
4 headrest rods	5′ × 1/2″	[1.5m × 1.3cm]
12–15 seat rods	3′ × 3/8″	[.9m × .95cm]
1 back arm support	18″ × 3/4″	[46 × 1.9cm]

Fig. 6-1. Child's chair, Greenbrier County, West Virginia.

Frame. Working on a low, level bench, line up one back post (A) and one front post (B), as shown in figure 6-2. Incline the back post to an angle of about eight degrees, or bend the post at the level of the seat rail. Nail two of the fifteen-inch [38cm] horizontal rails (C&D) in place, leaving a one-inch [2.5cm] overhang at each end. Place the lower rail (C) three inches [7.6cm] above the floor. Make up the other side of chair as a mirror image.

Stand the sides of chair upright and nail horizontal rails, E, F, G, and H to the upright posts. Nail the eighteen-inch [46cm] back arm support rail (I) to the back posts, halfway between the back seat rail (D) and the tops of the back posts. Nail remaining rails (J and K) to the seat rails.

Nail the tops of the diagonal braces (L) to the inside of the upper front leg. Before attaching braces to the inside of the back legs, stand the chair frame on a level surface and, if necessary, twist it until the legs are level. Trim all sharp edges of the rails with a penknife; add extra nails if necessary to steady the chair. The frame will not be completely sturdy until all of the flexible rods have been nailed in position.

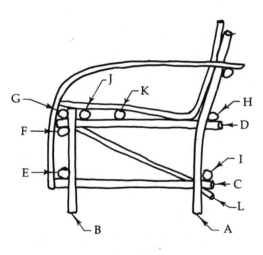

Fig. 6-2.

Arms. Arm rods should be cut within two days of construction. (If this is not possible, standing green rods in a large container of water will preserve their flexibility for a longer time.) Discard rods with knotholes. The diameter of the rods should average one-half inch [1.3cm]. Insert the butt of the first rod down behind lower front rung, about five inches [12.7cm] from the front post; nail the rod from inside the chair frame. Take the rod in front of the leg post, curve it about three inches [7.6cm] above the top of the post, and clamp the end to the back arm support with a metal spring clamp. Repeat with the second arm rod on the other side of the chair.

The tension in the bent arm rods will warp the chair frame. Make adjustments in both rods until the frame is again square and the lines of the curved arms are pleasing. Remove the clamps and nail the ends of the rods to the back arm support, close to the back posts. Trim the ends of the arm rods with pruning shears, not too close to the nails or the wood will split.

Working on alternate sides of the chair, add the other arm rods, one at a time, matching their outlines to the first pair. Keep rods parallel by tacking them with small brads every five or six inches [12.7–15.2cm]. (This can be accomplished, also, with a slender box nail of the proper length by driving the nail through the side of each rod as it is added, beginning from the inside of the first arm rod.)

After the arms have been completed, adjust them slightly and nail the eight rods, from the outside, to the front seat rail. (In an adult chair, the lower front rung should be made of seasoned wood and the rung should be nailed to the inside of the front leg posts. The tension in the arm rods will force a green rung to bend or to pull away from the chair frame.)

Headrest. Trim the tops of the back posts to a fifty-degree slope. (See fig. 6-1) Place the butt of a long rod down behind a side seat rail, three inches [7.6cm] from the front post. Bend the rod across the tops of the back posts and clamp the end to the seat rail on the other side of the chair. Adjust the curve before nailing. Nail the rod to the tops of the back posts. Add the remaining headrest rods, alternating butts on each side and inclining the rods slightly at top back toward the seat. Nail the rods parallel in a few places. Make final adjustments of curves and nail the headrest rods to the armrests.

Seat. Starting at the center front, nail a small three-eighths-inch [.95cm] withe flush with front seat rail to the tops of all seat rails. Allow the rear of the seat to sag slightly. Bend the rod slowly, but firmly, into position against the back seat support. Nail. Give rods a slight twist as you bend them to prevent cracking. Cut the top of the rod even with the second or third rod of the headrest. Brad it to the first rod of the headrest. Fill out the remaining seat space with small green rods placed about one-half inch [1.3cm] apart, taking care to keep the back curve of the seat level.

Split a 12″ × 3/4″ [30 × 1.9cm] rod in half with a penknife. Fit the piece of half-round against the front ends of the seat rods and nail it in several places. This smooth rod will protect the child's legs from the rough ends of the rods.

Allow the chair to season. Should splits develop in the nailed rods, glue and clamp the rods. *Drill* holes for new nails, should renailing be necessary.

Frame Dimensions for Adult-sized Chair

2 front posts	14″ × 1 1/2″	[35 × 3.8cm]
2 back posts	28″ × 1 1/2″	[70 × 3.8cm]
13 rails	21″ × 1″	[53.3 × 2.5cm]
10 arm rods	5′ × 3/4″	[1.5m × 1.9cm]
5 headrest rods	7′ × 3/4″	[2.1m × 1.9cm]
12–15 seat rods	4′ × 1/2″	[1.2m × 1.3cm]
1 back arm support	25″ × 1″	[63.5cm × 2.5cm]

A settee can be made by doubling the width of the seat. Add extra cross-bracing to the center of the seat frame.

Child's Chair in Willow

Precut

2 front posts	16 1/2″ × 1″ diameter	[42.3 × 2.5cm] (slightly splayed at seat level)
2 back posts	20″ × 1″	[50.8 × 2.5cm] (slightly splayed at seat level)
1 front seat rail	14″ × 1 1/4″	[35 × 3.1cm]
1 front rung	14″ × 1 1/4″	[35 × 3.1cm]
1 back seat rail	10 1/4″ × 1 1/4″	[26 × 3.1cm]
1 back rung	10 1/4″ × 1 1/4″	[26 × 3.1cm]
4 side rails	8 1/2″ × 1″	[21.6 × 2.5cm]
2 braces	12 1/2″ × 1/2″	[31.7 × 1.3cm]
3 back arm rail supports	14″ × 3/4″	[35 × 1.9 cm]
2 side arm rail supports	8 1/2″ × 3/4″	[21.6 × 1.9 cm]
4 seat rods (split)	10 1/2″ × 1 1/4″	[26.7 × 3.1cm]
2 flexible arm rails	46″ × 3/4″	[1.2m × 1.9cm]

Fig. 6-3. Willow and hickory child's chair, eastern Tennessee, ca. 1900.

Frame. Nail the front seat rail between the front posts. Seat height is ten and a half inches [26.7cm] from the floor. Nail the bottom front rung in position between the posts, three and a half inches [8.9cm] above the floor.

Nail the rear seat rail between the back posts. The rear seat height is ten inches [25.4cm] above the floor. Nail the back rung between the posts, three inches [7.6cm] above the floor.

Join the front and back sections, nailing so that the side rails are level with the rungs and seat rails. Stagger the nails to permit clearance. Place the chair frame on a level surface and square it. Nail cross braces on the inside to the top of the side seat rails and to the lower rear legs, on the inside. (Use fig. 6-1 as model since braces shown in fig. 6-3 were nailed incorrectly.)

Arms. Bend the arm rails gently to fit over the tops of the front and rear posts. Set aside. Saw the tops of the front posts to a slightly forward-sloping angle. Nail the rear arm rail supports in position to the side of the back seat rail. The top of the support should be eleven inches [27.9cm] above the seat rail. Allow the supports to slant about eight degrees toward the rear.

Place the butt end of one arm rod over top of the front post. Allow the rod to extend about three inches [7.6cm] beyond the post. Leaving space for the second rod, nail the rod to the top of the front post. Curving the rail, nail it in position to the tops of the rear posts and back supports, finishing up on the other front post. Reverse the taper of the second arm rail and, beginning on opposite side, curve the rod around on the outside of the first rail and nail it to the tops of all posts.

Nail the side arm rail supports in position to the side seat rails; then nail the arm rods to the tops of the supports. Trim the ends of the arm rails, with a sloping cut; the arm rods will extend two inches [5cm] over the front posts.

Seat. Split the rods for the seat and, if necessary to achieve an even thickness, plane the undersides with a drawknife. Position them on the tops of the seat rails, *drill* the nail holes, and tack the rods to the rails with small box nails.

Corduroy Table

Precut

4 legs	15″ × 1 1/2″ diameter	[38.1 × 3.8cm]
4 lower rungs	15″ × 1″	[38.1 × 2.5cm]
2 top rungs	13″ × 1″	[33 × 2.5cm]
2 support rails for top	18″ × 1 1/4″	[46 × 3.1cm]
8 cross braces	13 1/2″ × 1/2″	[33.8 × 3.8cm]
about 20 smooth, straight rods for tabletop	21 3/4″ × 3/4″	[55.2 × 1.9cm]

Make up two opposite sides. Nail the fifteen-inch [38.1cm] bottom rungs to the legs, three inches [7.6cm] above the floor; let the rungs extend one and a half inches [3.8cm] beyond the leg posts. Nail the short top rungs to the legs, one inch [2.5cm] below the tops of the leg posts. Permit the rungs to extend beyond the leg posts, as before.

Stand the sides upright and join by nailing the lower rungs to the leg posts, resting the rungs on top of the side rungs and extending them one and a half inches [3.8cm] beyond the legs. Center the two support rails for the top, place them above the upper side rungs, and nail them to the leg posts.

Tack the tops of the cross supports in position to the legs, as shown in figure 6-4, all around. Set the table base on a level surface to square it. Tack the lower ends of the cross braces to the legs, adjusting the squareness as each side is nailed.

Top. Alternate the taper of the rods for the top and align them on the top support rods. Center the rods, drill nail holes, and nail rods to supports. Split one rod to make two pieces of half-round moulding and nail them to the raw ends of the top, if desired.

Fig. 6-4. Corduroy-top table, Greenbrier County, West Virginia.

Bentwood Armchair

Fig. 6-5. Willow chair, Virginia, ca. 1920.

Frame. Rails and rungs for the undercarriage of the chair should be seasoned. The rods may be split in two, but the chair will be stronger if made with whole rods. The diagonal side braces should be split to streamline the exterior lines. All bentwood parts are to be made from freshly cut green wood. The curved seat rail may be set to shape on a form, but it is not required. Splayed legs can be selected from natural growth or bent on a brake.

Nail the lower front rung to the front posts, seven inches [17.8cm] from the floor. Nail the front seat rail to the posts, thirteen and a half inches [34.3cm] from the floor. Nail the back rung to the back posts, seven inches [17.8cm] above the floor. Tack scrap brace to the legs to give stability to the back section while the undercarriage is being constructed.

Stand the front and back sections upright and join them with the side rungs. Attach diagonal bracing, nailing it to the outside of the frame. (See fig. 6-7) The end of the upper rear brace (A) is nailed to the back post twelve and a half inches [31.3cm] above the floor.

Bend the curved seat rail and fit it into the framework, nailing it to the front and back posts from inside. *Drill* a hole for a long nail at the center back seat rail (B) and drive the nail well into seat support. Push the rear seat curve back hard and nail the opposite end of the support rod to the top of the front seat rail, flush with front edge.

Arms. Bend the arm rods, nail front ends six or seven inches [15.2–17.8cm] out from the legs on the front rung, curve to the back, and attach to the back rung. (See instructions for Child's Willow Chair, p. 97.) Nail the rods together every five or six inches [12.7–15.2cm], and nail, also, to the front and back posts. (Fig. 6-6)

Backrest. Fit the back struts in position and trim the tops of struts and back posts to accommodate the curve of the backrest. Nail the struts in position through bottom of the seat rail. Attach the first curved rod for the backrest and nail it to the back posts and to the struts with small finishing nails. (Fig. 6-7, point C) After the two remaining back rods have been added, drive long nails through all rods and into the tops of the struts and posts.

Seat. Beginning with the front edge of the seat, mark, cut, and nail the seat rods to the seat rail and to the center seat support. (Fig. 6-8) Allow a quarter-inch [.64cm] space between rods. After the seating rods have been nailed in place, bend the slender trim rod (D) and cover the nailed edges of the seat rods. Tack it to the seat rods in several places.

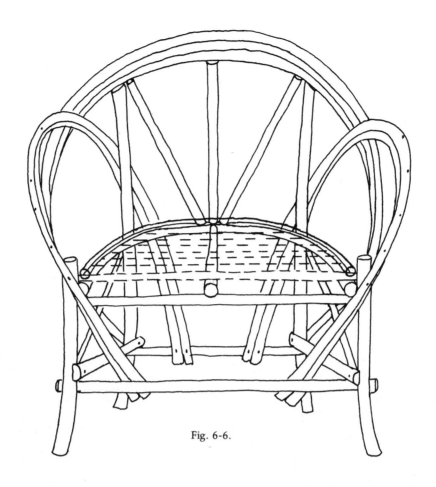

Fig. 6-6.

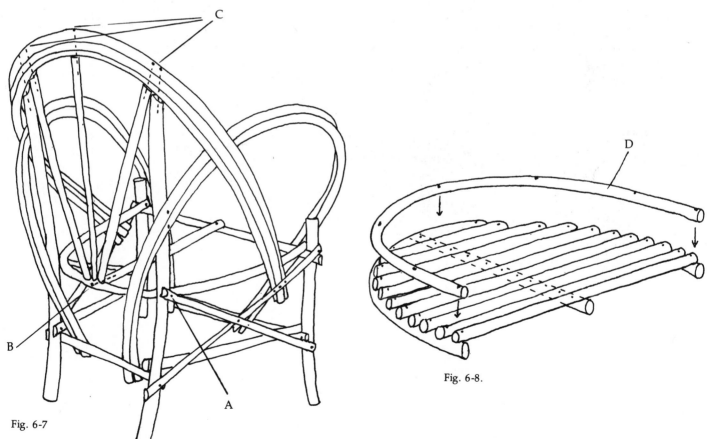

C

D

B

A

Fig. 6-7

Fig. 6-8.

Hickory or Oak Settee

The lengths of the horizontal rungs and rails are given as the inside measurements in Fig. 6-10. Add extra length to each end for tenons. The length of the tenons depends upon the diameter of the stock used for the vertical posts. A tenon should extend at least halfway through post. For example, if the post measures two inches [5cm] in diameter, the tenon should be one inch [2.5cm] long. The posts will have natural taper, so tenons and mortise holes will decrease slightly in length and depth as the post becomes narrower. Vertical measurements along the sides of the posts are measured on centers of mortise holes.

Ideally, this settee should be made with seasoned rungs and green posts; however, partially seasoned wood may be used exclusively provided finishing nails are driven through the tenons and into the posts. (See fig. 3-18, p. 87.)

Beginning with the back of the settee, assemble the rungs and stretchers for the woven seat back. Insert tenoned ends of this back panel, the seat rail, and the lower back rung into previously drilled mortise holes in one of the back posts. Fit the opposite ends into the other back post, turn the back section on its side, and hammer tenons into the posts with a hard rubber mallet, or use a scrap piece of leather over the bark and hammer the assembly with a stick of smooth wood. Protect the bark from direct blows of sharp or metal tools.

Assemble the front section of the settee. Stand the back of the settee against a wall. Set the front section against the back, centering both parts. Move the front section of the settee forward to the correct depth of seat. Have someone hold the section steady or tack scrap pieces of wood to the framework. Now, make a sight judgment of angles for mortise holes to be

Fig. 6-9. Rustic hickory furniture manufactured by the Old Hickory Chair Company, Martinsville, Indiana, ca. 1915. Center: rustic settee; left: hickory captain's chair; right: rocking chair.

drilled for side rungs and seat rails. Drill the seat rail mortises first. Remember that the back of the seat is one inch [2.5cm] lower than the front seat rail. Join the front and back sections with seat rails. Adjust the frame by twisting until it is reasonably square. Taking up an upper side rung, hold it against the outside front and back posts, level at proper height, and mark the level on each post with a colored crayon or pencil. Using a small try-square, transfer the marks to inside of the legs. (A semicircular cardboard template, marked with degrees, can be used to measure correct angles for mortises, but eyesight alone will be more efficient with irregularly shaped poles.) Work on alternate sides, fitting, measuring, and drilling holes. Add lower rungs.

Before fitting the armrests, hammer the side joints. Set the armrests in place over the tenons of the top front posts; mark and drill a mortise in the back post, fit the tenon in place, and mark the location for a mortise underneath the forward end of the arm. After the armrests have been fitted, knock loose the front section of the seat, position the arms over the ends of the front posts, place opposite tenons into the back posts, and hammer front and back sections together,

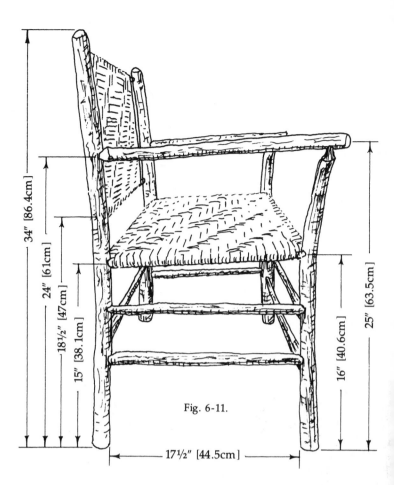

Fig. 6-11.

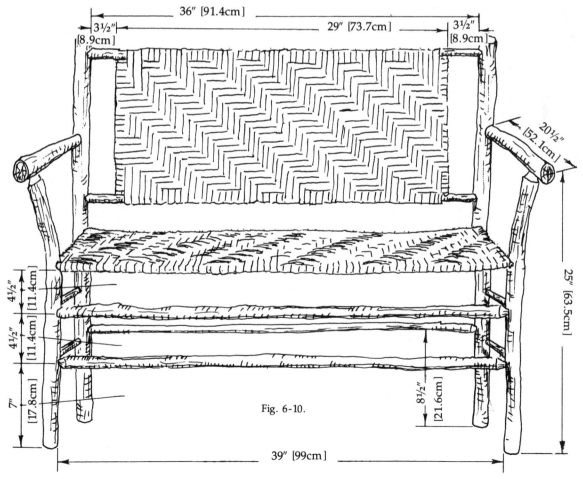

Fig. 6-10.

Fig. 6-12.

working on alternate sides to permit frame to adjust to square. If settee is warped, tap offending tenons to loosen them slightly or shave a small amount of stock from them with a penknife. Refit the tenons until the frame is satisfactory, then drive nails into tenons and posts. A final adjustment of leveling the legs (fig. 6-12), should it be necessary, should not be made until after the seat and back have been woven with splints or with wide seating cane.

The procedure given above entails a good bit of trial-and-error fitting, and the first settee built in this fashion will be tedious for the builder. In time, however, the craftsperson will develop shortcuts rather quickly and will be able to make rapid sight judgments of angles.

Figures 6-13 and 6-14 give measurements for a hickory chair. The finished product will resemble the rocking chair in figure 6-9 without the rockers.

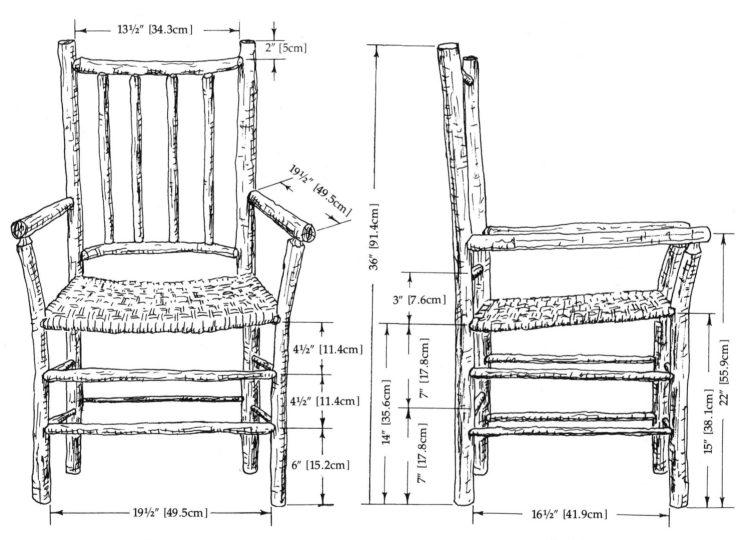

Fig. 6-13.

Fig. 6-14.

Hickory Captain's Chair

The base of the rustic captain's chair is constructed according to the same general directions given for the settee. The bentwood arm and back supports, made of green hickory or white oak, are not added until the tenons of the base have been nailed, and preferably not until the seat has been woven. The green rods will exert considerable pressure against the posts, especially if more than two rods are used. The rods may be set to the proper curvature in a bending form, if desired. (See page 84.)

Cut two (or more) slender saplings. The lower rod will be about fifty-four inches [1.4m] long before the tenons are trimmed, and the top rod will be about sixty-six inches [1.7m] long. Total length will depend upon the amount of splay in the back posts. Beginning with the lower rod, cut a tenon on the butt end. Make preliminary bends all along the length of the rod by bending the rod around a large tree. Fit the rod in position and note the angle for the position of the mortise in the front post. Drill mortise, insert tenon; fit the rod to the inside of the chair frame, and sight the angle for a mortise in the opposite front post. Trim the end of the rod, if necessary, and cut the tenon. Fit the tenoned ends of the rod into the posts, push the rod down firmly against the back posts, adjust the curved shape of the rod and nail the rod to each of the back posts. Repeat with the top rod, reversing the butt end of the rod to prevent undue tension on one side of the chair. Nail tenons at front posts. Weave the seat back.

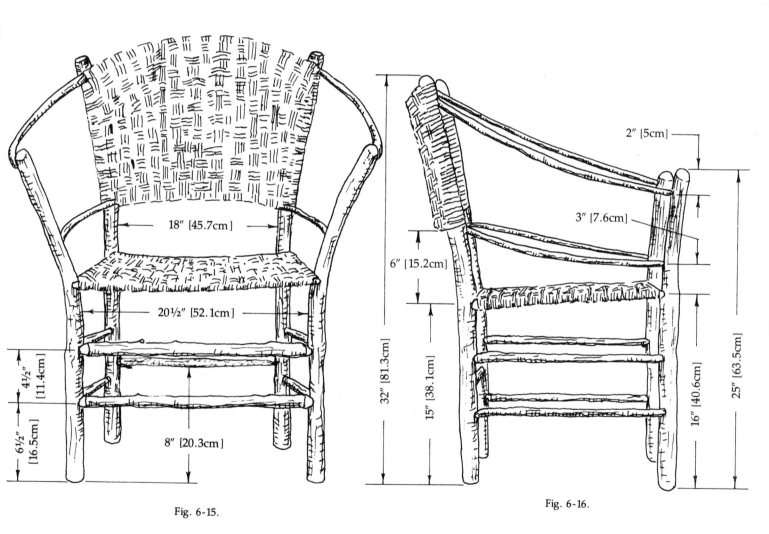

Fig. 6-15.

Fig. 6-16.

An Adjustable Rustic Daybed

A major requirement for this daybed will be two nearly identical young trees, each containing a natural offset, to be used for the posts of the adjustable back-rest. The offset is necessary to allow the back assembly to be level with the seat when the back is in the reclining positions. To adjust the back, lift the back frame entirely out of the seat, flip it over, and reinsert it into the seat so that the foot will lodge behind the stretcher either at point B or at point C in figure 6-18.

U-branched pear trees are perfect sources for the back posts, but it is not uncommon to find wild young saplings with this sort of offset form in the lower branches. If both branches of the U are still intact, cut off one of them at the crotch and round the saw cut with a wood rasp.

The construction of the bed is a straightforward mortise-and-tenon stool construction. (Measurement allowance must be made for side clearance of the back assembly, depending upon the size and taper of the back posts.) After the seat and the back have been built, insert the back into the seat frame, lodging legs behind stretcher at point A (fig. 6-18). Push the seat forward until it touches the rear seat rail at point D. Permit the back to drop back about a half inch [1.3cm], or so; mark the positions on the rear seat legs for peg holes at point E. The back will rest against the pegs, but also it must be able to be lifted clear of the frame. The position of the pegs will depend upon the thickness and the curvature of the offset in the back posts. Remove the backrest, drill peg holes, and drive three-quarter-inch [1.9cm] round pegs, about five inches [12.7cm] long, into the legs.

Build the bed with seasoned wood. See pages 94-95 for instructions on seat weaving.

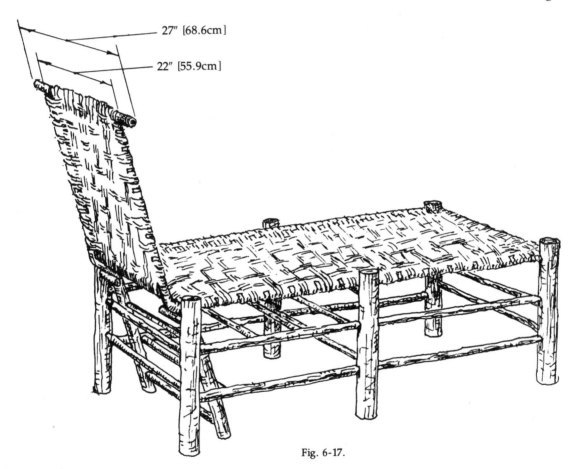

27″ [68.6cm]

22″ [55.9cm]

Fig. 6-17.

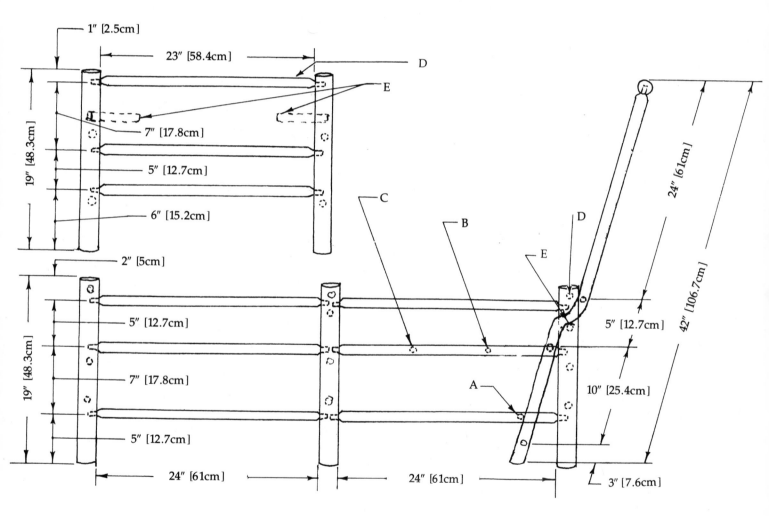

Fig. 6-18.

CHAPTER 7

Pergolas and Summerhouses

Before the advent of air conditioning, devices for keeping cool in the heat of summer were many and varied. In an age short on electrical energy, it is time to revive some of these techniques on a large scale. The vine-covered pergola, for example, is as ancient as artificially constructed grottoes. The temperature beneath a large, leafy pergola can be ten to fifteen degrees cooler in a torrid setting. Unfortunately, it takes several years to create a pergola. It's well worth the time, however, since a mature pergola will serve as protection against heat *and* rain. Because of the weight of the vines and the time required to grow and to care for the plants, it is a mistake to use wood for the scaffolding. Metal pipes will be more durable. Rustic poles can be split and laid across the top lattice to soften the stark, bare framework until the vines have begun to grow across the top. The idea is to grow a dense mat of vines and leaves across the top of the pergola.

Two or three varieties of woody climbing plants and rapidly growing slender vines of luxuriant growth are planted at the bases of the supports and trained up the poles. In the past, pergolas were often attached to the entire rear or side wall of a house and allowed to extend twenty to thirty feet [6–9m] into the lawn. Their ceilings should be high, to allow air to circulate, and, ideally, they should be placed in the path of prevailing wind currents.

A pergola attached to a house can easily become a summer living room, but pergolas need not be confined to private homes. Shopping malls and restaurants, for example, could make use of large pergolas in the summer months. The only hazard will be bees during the blooming season. Some variety of evergreen vine should be included for color during the winter months. Hanging baskets containing ivy can be suspended from the top lattice for a few years, if the climate will allow.

Smaller summerhouses lend picturesque charm to gardens and they are useful constructions for entertainment as well. Unless straw thatch is used as roofing material, they will not be so cool as a pergola. Regrettably, the Western world has, at the moment, a dearth of thatchers (and thatching straw). Thatch is simple to apply to a roof, however, and included at the end of this chapter are instructions for sewing a thatched roof of the most basic type.

Plans for building a rustic summerhouse requiring some prior building experience are given on pages 112–15, figures 7-7 through 7-10. Another summerhouse, requiring little or no building expertise, can be constructed by setting into the ground, about two feet [61cm] deep, the ends of locust (or other decay-resistant wood) poles in an octagonal or hexagonal shape around the perimeter of a tree. (See fig. 2-9, p. 44.) Nail a lattice of irregular twigs and branches to the poles; nail plate logs across the tops of the locust poles; and notch and fit the overhanging rafters for the roof to the plates, attaching the other ends to the tree with nails. (A few nails will not harm the tree.) Thatch the roof, plant vines to cover it, or use conventional wood or composition shingles. A shaggy-looking roof for a summerhouse can be made by covering roofing paper with sticky tar and sprinkling pine needles on the tar. Work directly on the roof, section by section.

Andrew Jackson Downing gives instructions for creating a moss house in *Landscape Gardening and Rural Architecture* (1841). Poles for the house are set up as above. A lath of half-inch [1.3 cm] rods with the bark intact is nailed to the posts about three-quarters of an inch [2.5 cm] apart, and clumps of soft woods moss are then stuffed between the lath rods with a small wooden wedge. The rods will be completely covered by the spread-out tufts of moss. Downing states that the moss will retain its green color for "a great length of time."[1]

Thatching

The long stems of many plants are covered with natural waterproofing. When bundles of these stems are arranged in parallel order and attached to battens nailed across the rafters of a steeply pitched roof (at least four or five [10.2–12.7cm] inches per each foot [30cm] of rise), rainwater will run off the material instead of soaking into it. The best way to understand a thatched roof is to think of the bundles of straw, called *yealms*, as thick shingles. Yealms of straw are applied to a roof in the same way that shingles are. Working in courses from the eaves toward the top, one overlaps each course in a stepwise progression. Simple long straw thatching, tied onto the battens with tarred or nylon cord, is quite easy to do, but locating the straw is another matter.

Thatch should be lightweight and waterproof. Hollow straw from long-stemmed wheat or rye is ideal; in order to retain its natural resistance to water, how-ever, the outer covering of the hollow stem must not be broken or crushed. Modern threshing machines were not designed to preserve the straw by-product for thatching roofs; consequently, the would-be thatcher will have to obtain his straw by hand-cutting his own half-acre of grain with a scythe and cradle, if he can find one. In addition to this labor, he will have to remove the grain, not with a flail, which will crush the straw, but by brushing the seed heads, handful by handful, against a paling fence or some such contrived framework. If the grain is not removed, the summerhouse roof will have birds and rodents as permanent guests or, worse, the roof will ferment.

Long-stemmed wheat has been bred almost out of existence. A variety called "red top" has fairly long stems that appear to be very tough. Depending upon the soil, rye straw will average three and a half to four feet [1–1.2m] in length. Certain sedge grasses can be used for thatch, as well as palm leaves, Norfolk reed (*Phragmites communis*), river cane (*Arundinaria tecta*), bamboo, and marsh grasses such as cattail leaves and rush; nonetheless, long-stemmed grain straw (the longer the stems, the easier the work and the better the roof) will be the best and most durable material to use with the particular thatching technique described below.

The grain is cut about a week before its normal harvest, while the lower stems still have some green color. It should be put into small upright shocks, tied loosely with binder's twine or a twist of straw, and allowed to dry for two or three weeks in the field. After the grain has been removed, and the day before the thatching, the bundles should be spread out on the ground and sprayed lightly with a garden hose. The straw is easier to handle if it is slightly damp during the thatching. Now, the straw is formed into yealms and tied, ready for the roof. Handle the straw carefully; keep the stems parallel; comb it, if necessary, with the fingers or with a paddlelike comb (fig. 7-1) made by driving nails, an inch apart, through a piece of one-by-two [2.5 × 5cm]. Figure 7-2 shows a simple yealm former, cut from the crotch of a young tree, which can also double as a carrier if the thatcher chooses to make up yealms as he goes along. The yealm should be four to six inches [10.2–15.2cm] thick and fourteen to eighteen inches [35–46cm] wide. The butts of the straw should be tamped level against the ground before being added to the form. It is easier to make up the yealms ahead of time.

Battens made of narrow planed stock or split one-and-one-half-inch [3.8cm] hardwood rods (bark intact) should be nailed across the rafters about eight to ten inches [20–25.4cm] apart. The distance between the battens depends upon the length of the straw. Each yealm will need to be tied to each of two battens, and three ties to three battens will be even better.[2]

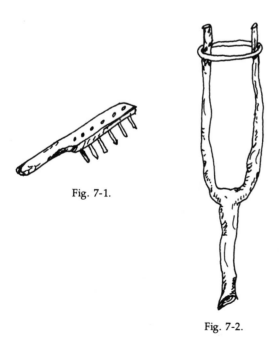

Fig. 7-1.

Fig. 7-2.

For sewing the straw onto the battens, a two-foot-long [61cm] thatcher's needle will be required. The needle can be made up by a blacksmith or a machine shop from a slender metal rod. One end of the rod is flattened and drilled for an eye and the other end is flattened and pointed. (Fig. 7-3) The twine should be a good grade of marlin cord, tarred cord, or some weather-resistant synthetic fiber cord. Another worker will be needed on the inside of the roof, to receive the threaded needle, to tie off the cord around the battens with a slip knot, and to pass the needle back up to the worker on the roof.

The thatching begins at the eaves with *double* thickness yealms (to give a dense eave line, which will be trimmed with shears after the roof has been completed). The butts of the yealms are allowed to extend about four inches [10.2cm] below the lowest batten, and the thick yealm is sewed and tied onto the batten about every four or five inches [10.2–12.7cm] across the width of the bundle. On this first eave course, the tips of the heavy yealms will spring up into the air unless they are battened down temporarily with a scrap of wood or tied for the moment with twine. If the thatcher does not mind the awkwardness of the situation, they can simply be allowed to stick up in

the air. Once the second course is laid over the tips of the yealms, the problem will be solved.

The second course of yealms (fig. 7-4) is laid over the first, with the butts extending an inch or two [2.5–5cm] over the stitching on the first course. This course is tied to the second batten, the needle penetrating both layers of the first and second courses.

The thatching proceeds, course by course, in this manner until the peak of the conical roof is reached. At the peak, toenail an eighteen-inch [46cm] rod of wood to the peak of the rafters, gather the thinned ends of the straw around the slender stake, and bind the topknot with cord and fasten off. (Fig. 7-5) A miniature birdhouse, also having a thatched roof, can be nailed to the top of the stake, or a weather vane or some such decorative ornament made either from straw or wood can be attached to the peak of the roof.

Smooth and flatten the straw over the roof to give it a uniform appearance and to conceal the joining of the yealms. Comb the straw lightly, if necessary. The soffit, or under edge of the eaves, will now be given a sort of crew cut. Hedge shears, a sharp knife, or electrical hedge trimmers may be used. The straw eaves should be almost parallel with the ground and very evenly cut.

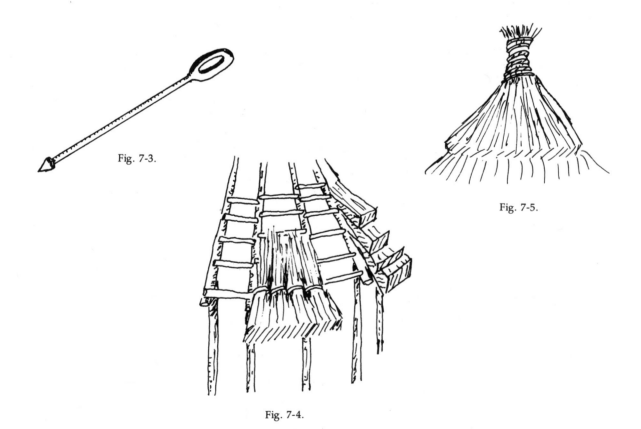

Fig. 7-3.

Fig. 7-5.

Fig. 7-4.

110

The Summerhouse Plans

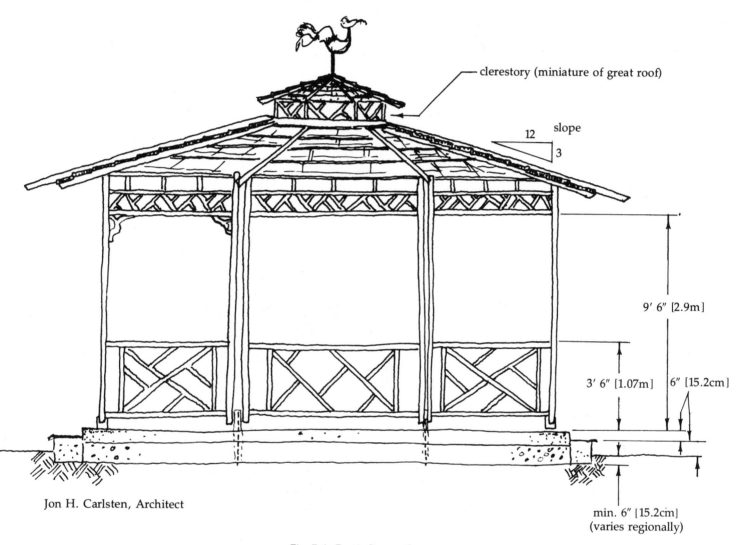

clerestory (miniature of great roof)

slope
12
3

9' 6" [2.9m]

3' 6" [1.07m]

6" [15.2cm]

Jon H. Carlsten, Architect

min. 6" [15.2cm]
(varies regionally)

Fig. 7-6. Rustic Summerhouse

Section/Elevation

Scale
¼" = 1'
[.63cm = 30.5cm]

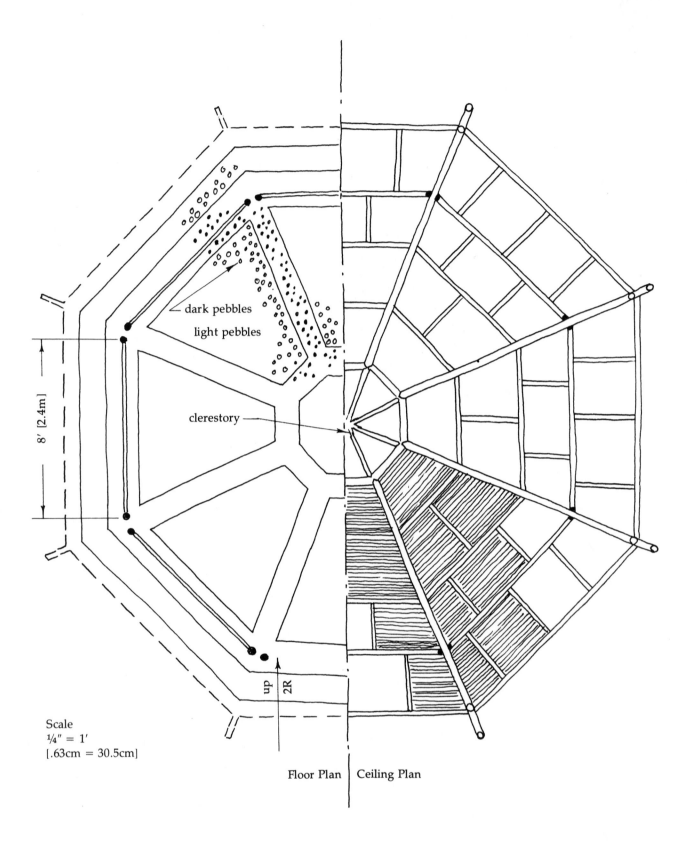

dark pebbles

light pebbles

clerestory

8' [2.4m]

up 2R

Scale
1/4" = 1'
[.63cm = 30.5cm]

Floor Plan | Ceiling Plan

Fig. 7-7.

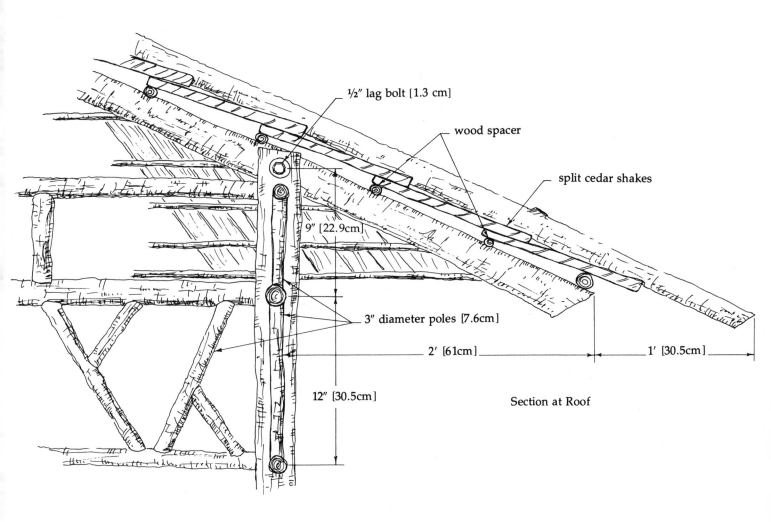

½″ lag bolt [1.3 cm]

wood spacer

split cedar shakes

9″ [22.9cm]

3″ diameter poles [7.6cm]

2′ [61cm]

1′ [30.5cm]

12″ [30.5cm]

Section at Roof

Fig. 7-8.

Scale   1¾″ = 1′

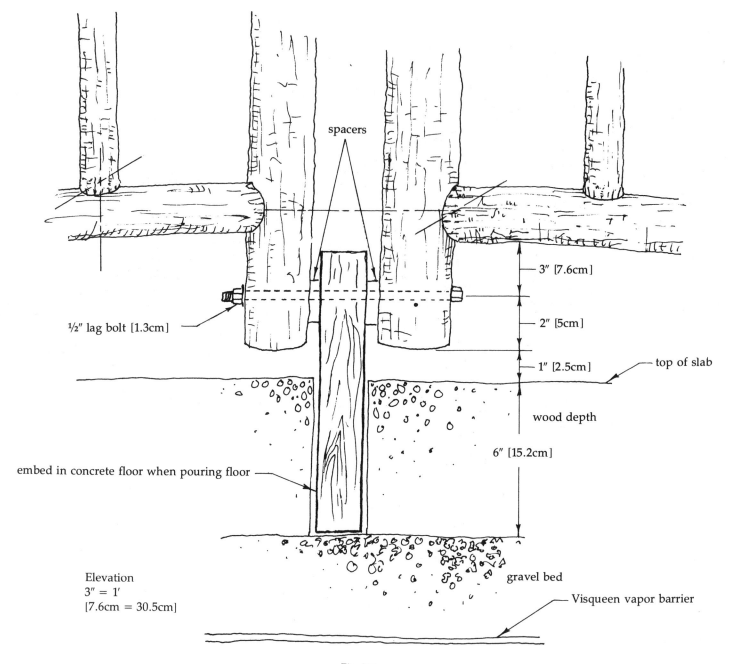

spacers

½″ lag bolt [1.3cm]

3″ [7.6cm]

2″ [5cm]

1″ [2.5cm]

top of slab

wood depth

6″ [15.2cm]

embed in concrete floor when pouring floor

Elevation
3″ = 1′
[7.6cm = 30.5cm]

gravel bed

Visqueen vapor barrier

Fig. 7-9.

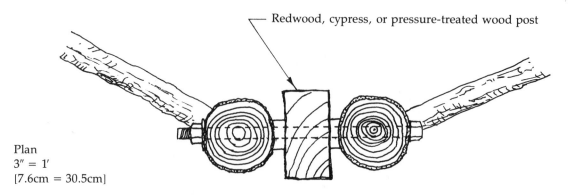

Redwood, cypress, or pressure-treated wood post

Plan
3″ = 1′
[7.6cm = 30.5cm]

Fig. 7-10.

114

CHAPTER 8

Miscellaneous Designs

Chairs and Seats

In the following pages will be found some design ideas, drawn from many sources, to assist the rustic furniture maker who wishes to go beyond the patterns and instructions provided and to employ the materials of Nature. Several of the chair designs make use of strong natural crotches. Crotches in trees are engineered by Nature to support the heavy weight of limbs and leaves and they are, as a consequence, ideal for rustic furniture.

If the designer will keep in mind the principles and the techniques outlined in Chapter 3 and if he or she will make an active search for the design inherent in the growing tree, the possibilities for creating an interesting piece of natural furniture are almost limitless.

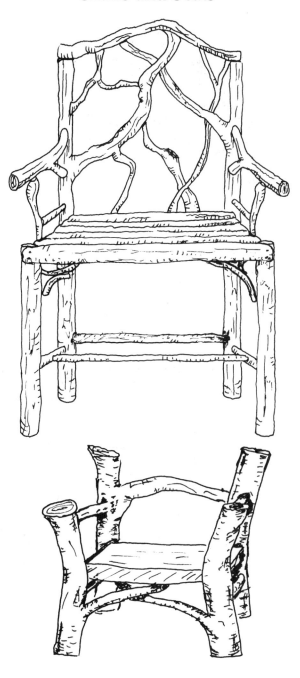

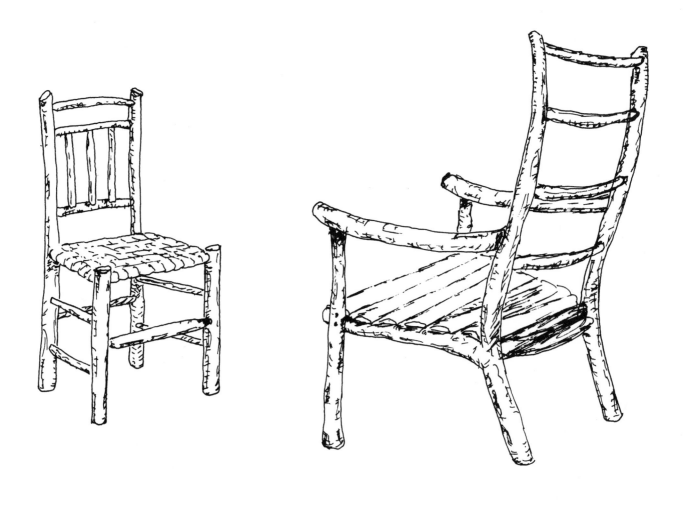

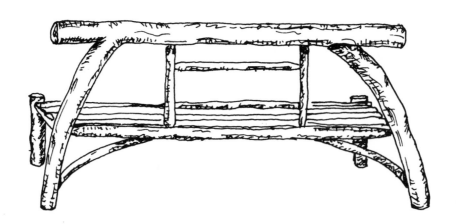

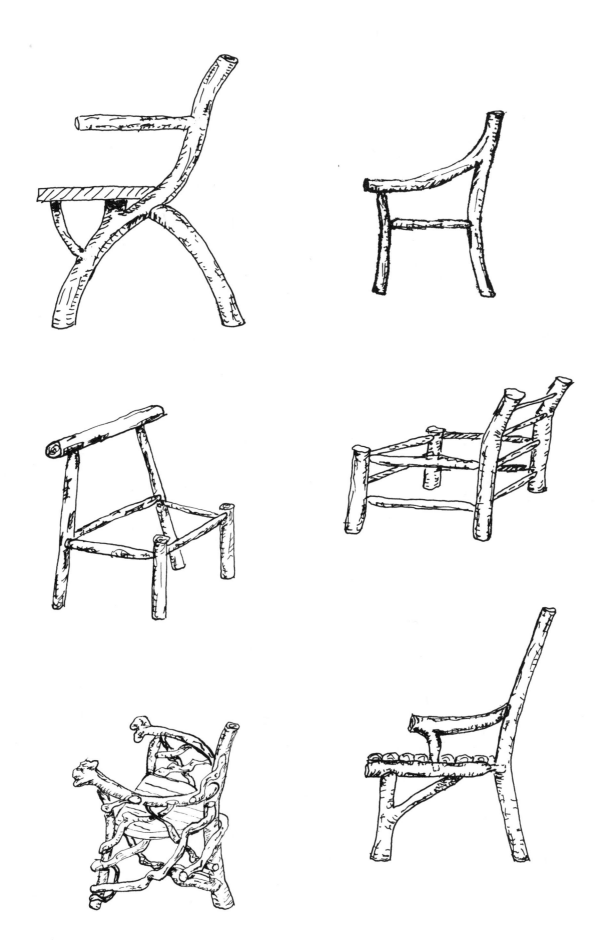

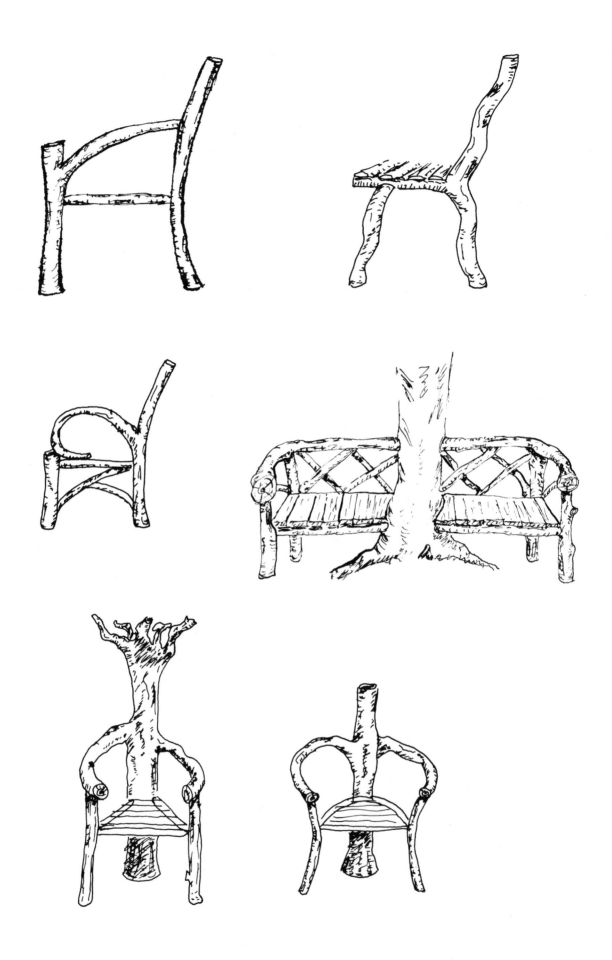

Beds

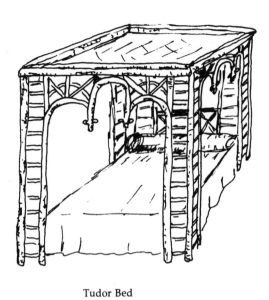

Tudor Bed

"Chippendale Bed"

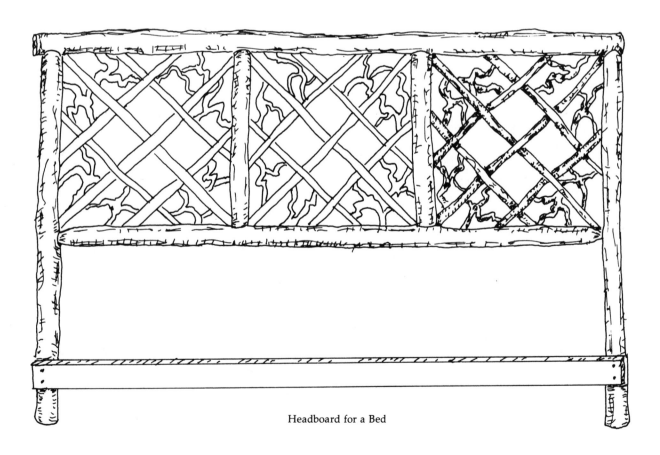

Headboard for a Bed

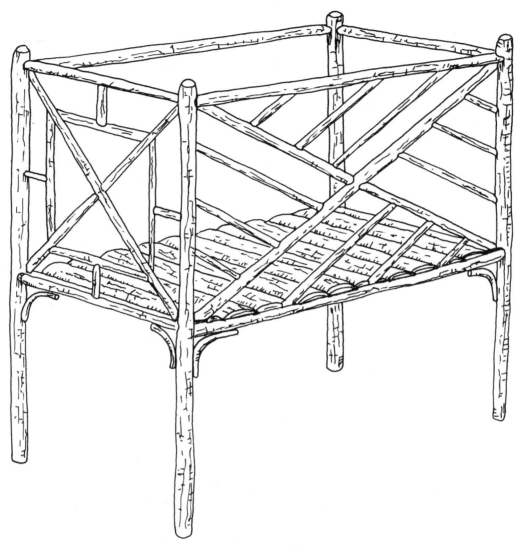

Child's Crib

Sources of Supply

Peerless Rattan and Reed Manufacturing Company, Inc.
97 Washington Street
New York, New York 10006
    Rattan cane and hand-rived white-ash splints

The H.H. Perkins Company
10 South Bradley Road
Woodbridge, Connecticut 06525
    Rattan cane and white-oak splints

Notes

Chapter 1: The Eighteenth Century

1. Marie Luise Gothein, *A History of Garden Art*, ed. Walter P. Wright, 2 vols. (London: J. M. Dent and Sons, 1928), II: 284, 285.

2. Horizon Magazine, eds., *The Horizon Book of the Arts of China* (New York: American Heritage Publishing Co., 1969), p. 369.

3. Elizabeth Gilmore Holt, ed., *A. Documentary History of Art*, 2 vols., 2d ed. (Garden City, New York: Doubleday and Co., 1957–58), I: 301.

4. Ibid., p. 297.

5. Georgina Masson, *Italian Gardens* (London: Thames and Hudson, 1966), p. 13.

6. Wolfgang Kayser, *The Grotesque in Art and Literature*, trans. Ulrich Weisstein (Bloomington: Indiana University Press, 1963), p. 19.

7. The latinized form of *topia, topiarius*, was used to designate a gardener who specialized in creating miniature gardens by clipping trees and shrubs and training ivy. Cicero complimented his brother's gardener, the *topiarius*, in a letter written in 54 B.C. See Masson, pp. 15, 16.

8. John Ruskin, *Works*, eds. E. T. Cook and Alexander Wedderburn, vol. XI: *The Stones of Venice* (New York: Longmans Green and Co., 1903–12), p. 170.

9. Richard Brilliant, *Roman Art* (London: Phaidon Press, 1974), pp. 33, 34.

10. A photograph of a pastoral grotto scene, created by Giovanni da Bologna, is shown in Franzsepp Wörtenberger, *Mannerism*, trans. Michail Heron (New York: Holt, Rinehart and Winston, 1963), p. 64.

11. Gothein, I: 286.

12. Masson, pp. 193, 194.

13. Masson describes a grotto in an Italian garden (Giardino Buonaccorsi) "peopled with Baroque figures of friars in attitudes of ecstasy." From a concealed niche in the wall, a devil suddenly emerges to startle the spectator. See Masson, p. 220.

14. Gothein, I: 362.

15. Warren E. Cox, *Pottery and Porcelain*, 2 vols. (New York: Crown Publishers, 1970), I: 402–405.

16. Gothein, I: 417.

17. The creation of roomlike enclosures and covered avenues by means of pleaching tree limbs—that is, by interweaving the limbs of tall trees—was used as a form of topiary in gardens of the Middle Ages.

18. Gothein, I: 453, 454.

19. John Aubrey, *Aubrey's Brief Lives*, ed. Oliver Lawson Dick (Ann Arbor: University of Michigan Press, 1957), p. 145.

20. Ibid., p. 44.

21. Ernst Kris, *Psychoanalytic Explorations in Art* (New York: International Universities Press, 1952), p. 213.

22. Annie Reich, "The Structure of the Grotesque-Comic Sublimation," *Bulletin of the Menninger Clinic* XIII (1949), pp. 160–171.

23. B. Sprague Allen, *Tides in English Taste*, 2 vols. (New York: Rowman and Littlefield, 1969), II: 135–137.

24. Kris, pp. 50–52.

25. John Gloag, *The Englishman's Chair* (London: Geoge Allen and Unwin, 1964), p. 149.

26. Alvar di Gonzalez-Palacios, *Il Mobile nei Secoli*, 10 vols. (Milan: Fratelli Fabri Editore, 1969), II: 5–11.

27. Gloag, pp. 183–198.

28. Robert Austin and Koichiro Ueda, *Bamboo* (New York: Weatherhill, 1970), p. 49.

29. For a description of the construction of Kublai Khan's summerhouse, held together with "two hundred cords of silk," see Marco Polo, *The Travels of Marco Polo* (New York: Horace Liveright, 1926), p. 106.

30. Gothein, II: 251.

Chapter 2: The Nineteenth and Early Twentieth Centuries

1. *The Oxford Book of Eighteenth Century Verse* (Oxford: The Clarendon Press, 1926), pp. 317–319.

2. Ibid., p. 319.

3. B. Sprague Allen, *Tides in English Taste*, II: 204.

4. Robert Southey ["Don Manuel Espriella"], *Letters from England* (1807), quoted in Allen, II: 206.

5. John Ives Sewall, *A History of Western Art* (New York: Henry Holt and Co., 1953), pp. 295–298.

6. Ibid., pp. 467–472.

7. John Ruskin, *Works*, VIII: *The Seven Lamps of Architecture*, pp. 252, 255.

8. John Ruskin, *Works*, XII: *Lectures on Architecture and Painting*, p. 62.

9. Richard Brown, *Domestic Architecture* (London: Bernard Quaritch, 1842), p. 256.

10. Edmund Bartell, Jun., *Hints for Picturesque Improvements in Ornamental Cottages* (London: J. Taylor, 1804), p. 77.

11. Edward Kemp, *How to Lay Out a Garden or Landscape Gardening* 2d ed. (New York: Wiley and Halsted, 1858), p. 310.

12. Thomas Tileston Waterman, *The Mansions of Virginia, 1706–1776* (New York: Bonanza Books, 1945); pp. 226–229.

13. Agnes Addison, *Romanticism and the Gothic Revival* (New York: Richard R. Smith, 1938), p. 131.

14. Fiske Kimball, *Thomas Jefferson, Architect* (Boston: privately printed, 1916), p. 169.

15. "Peregrine Prolix" [Philip Holbrook Nicklin], *Letters Descriptive of the Virginia Springs* 2d ed. (Philadelphia: H. S. Tanner, 1837), p. 20.

16. John Edward Caldwell, *A Tour Through Part of Virginia in the Summer of 1808. . . .* (Belfast: Smyth and Lyons, 1810), reprint ed. by William M. E. Rachal (Richmond: The Dietz Press, 1951).

17. Martha Norburn Mead, *Asheville . . . in Land of the Sky* (Richmond: The Dietz Press, 1942), p. 47

18. Kenneth Clark, *The Gothic Revival* (New York: Charles Scribner's Sons, 1929), pp. 150–174.

19. John Preston Arthur, *A History of Watauga County, North Carolina* (Richmond: Everett Waddey Co., 1915), p. 80.

20. Ibid., p. 81.

21. Susan Fenimore Cooper, *William West Skiles, A Sketch of Missionary Life at Valle Crucis in Western North Carolina, 1842–1862* (New York: James Pott and Co., 1890), p. 5.

22. Ibid., p. 58.

23. Andrew Jackson Downing, *Rural Essays* (New York: Leavitt and Allen, 1858), p. 111.

24. Fredrika Bremer, *Homes of the New World*, 2 vols. (New York: Harper and Brothers, 1853), I: 46.

25. Nicholas B. Wainwright, ed., *A Philadelphia Perspective: The Diary of Sidney George Fisher Covering the Years 1834–1871* (Philadelphia: The Historical Society of Pennsylvania, 1967), p. 201.

26. Cooper, p. 58.

27. John Steegman, *Victorian Taste* (Cambridge, MA: MIT Press, 1971), pp. 310–316.

28. Ruskin, *Works*, XI: *The Stones of Venice*, pp. 164, 165.

29. Ibid., p. 152.

30. Steegman, p. 315.

31. *The Nation* (February 28, 1867), (March 14, 1867).

32. Laura Wood Roper, *Frederick Law Olmstead* (Baltimore: Johns Hopkins University Press, 1973), pp. 291–302.

33. The settee is illustrated in Robert Bishop, *The American Chair, 1640–1970* (New York: E. P. Dutton and Co., 1972), p. 404.

34. Gothein, *History of Garden Art*, II: 428.

35. Richard Saunders, *Collecting and Restoring Wicker Furniture* (New York: Crown Publishers, 1976), p. 16.

36. Cleveland Amory, *The Last Resorts* (New York: Harper Brothers, 1948), p. 23

37. *The Greenbrier Heritage: White Sulphur Springs, West Virginia* (Haarlem: Arndt, Preston, Chapin, Lamb and Keen, n.d.), p. 53.

38. Quoted in Amory, pp. 204, 205.

39. Meade Minnigerode, *The Fabulous Forties* (New York: G. P. Putnam's Sons, 1924), p. 80.

40. Craig Gilborn, "Rustic Furniture in the Adirondacks, 1875–1925," *Antiques* (June 1976), p. 1218.

41. A drawing of this chair can be seen in a watercolor by J. W. Champney (1843–1903), *Artist in His Studio*, illustrated in *The M. and M. Karolik Collection of American Watercolors and Drawings, 1800–1875*, 2 vols. (Boston: Museum of Fine Arts, 1962), I: 101.

42. See illustrations of the "Spanish chairs" in Celia Jackson Otto, *American Furniture of the Nineteenth Century* (New York: Viking Press, 1956), p. 21.

43. Sue H. Stephenson, *Basketry of the Appalachian Mountains* (New York: Van Nostrand Reinhold Co., 1977), p. 28.

44. Private correspondence with Craig Gilborn.

45. Werner P. Friederich, *Outline of Comparative Literature* (Chapel Hill: University of North Carolina Press, 1954), p. 303.

46. See Kris, *Psychoanalytic Explorations in Art*, p. 175. ("In wit the matter is known and the manner is secret; in riddles, the manner is known and the matter to be discovered.")

Chapter 3: The Technology

1. Ernest Joyce, *The Encyclopedia of Furniture Making* (New York: Drake Publishers, 1970), pp. 103–111.

Chapter 4: Design

1. Franklin H. Gottshall, *Design for the Craftsman* (Milwaukee: Bruce Publishing Co., 1940). Much of the material in this chapter is drawn from this book, an excellent source for the beginning designer in furniture and ironwork.

2. John Gloag, *The Englishman's Chair*, p. 3.

Chapter 7: Pergolas and Summerhouses

1. Andrew Jackson Downing, *Landscape Gardening and Rural Architecture* (New York: Wiley and Putnam, 1841), p. 459.

2. Phebe Westcott Humphreys, *The Practical Book of Garden Architecture* (Philadelphia: J. B. Lippincott Co., 1914), pp. 278–287.

A Selected Bibliography

Entries marked with an asterisk (*) are main sources used for the background social history.

Addison, Agnes. *Romanticism and the Gothic Revival*. New York: Richard R. Smith, 1938.

*Allen, B. Sprague. *Tides in English Taste*. 2 vols. New York: Rowman and Littlefield, 1969.

*Amory, Cleveland. *The Last Resorts*. New York: Harper and Brothers, 1948.

*Appleton, William W. *A Cycle of Cathay*. New York: Columbia University Press, 1961.

Arthur, John Preston. *A History of Watauga County, North Carolina*. Richmond: Everett Waddley Co., 1915.

Arts and Crafts Essays by members of the Arts and Crafts Exhibition Society. Preface by William Morris. London: Longmans Green and Co., 1903.

*Aubrey, John. *Aubrey's Brief Lives*. Edited from the original manuscripts and with a *Life of John Aubrey* by Oliver Lawson Dick. Ann Arbor: University of Michigan Press, 1957.

Austen, Jane. *The Complete Novels of Jane Austen: Sense and Sensibility*. New York: Modern Library, n.d.

Austin, Robert and Ueda, Koichiro with photographs by Dana Levy. *Bamboo*. New York: Weatherhill, 1970.

Bartell, Edmund, Jun. *Hints for Picturesque Improvements in Ornamental Cottages*. London: J. Taylor, 1804.

Bishop, Robert. *The American Chair, 1640–1970*. New York: E. P. Dutton and Co., 1972.

*Blackmun, Ora. *Western North Carolina: Its Mountains and Its People to 1880*. Boone, North Carolina: Appalachian Consortium Press, 1977.

*Blondel, Jacques Francois (1705–1774). *Extraits de la distribution des maisons de plaisance* . . . Paris: Armand Guerinet, n.d.

Bøe, Alf. *From Gothic Revival to Functional Form*. Oslo: Oslo University Press, 1957.

Bowen, Catherine Drinker. *Francis Bacon: The Temper of a Man*. Boston: Little, Brown and Co., 1963.

Bramwell, Martyn, ed. *The International Book of Wood*. New York: Simon and Schuster, 1976.

*Bremer, Fredrika. *Homes of the New World*. Mary Howitt, trans. 2 vols. New York: Harper and Brothers, 1853.

Brilliant, Richard. *Roman Art*. London: Phaidon Press, 1974.

*Brooks, Van Wyck. *The World of Washington Irving*. New York: E. P. Dutton and Co., 1944.

Brown, Richard. *Domestic Architecture*. London: Bernard Quaritch, 1842.

Brumbaugh, Robert S. *Ancient Greek Gadgets and Machines*. New York: Thomas Y. Crowell Co., 1966.

*Burckhardt, Jacob. *The Civilization of the Renaissance in Italy*. London: Phaidon Press, 1944.

*Burke, Edmund. *Works*. London: G. Bell and Sons, 1913.

*Caldwell, John Edwards. *A Tour Through Part of Virginia in the Summer of 1808 and also Some Account of the Islands in the Atlantic Ocean Known by the Name of the Azores*. Belfast: Smyth and Lyons, 1810. Reprint edition, Wm. M. E. Rachal, ed. Richmond: Dietz Press, 1951.

*Cameron, Nigel. *Barbarians and Mandarins*. Chicago: University of Chicago Press, 1970.

Carmer, Carl. *The Hudson*. New York: Farrar and Rinehart, 1939.

Cescinsky, Herbert. *English Furniture from Gothic to Sheraton*. Reprint edition. New York: Dover Publications, 1968.

Chippendale, Thomas. *The Gentleman and Cabinet-maker's Director*. . . 3d ed. London: for the author, 1762.

*Clark, Kenneth. *The Gothic Revival*. New York: Charles Scribner's Sons, 1929.

————. *Landscape into Art*. London: John Murray, 1949.

Coleridge, Anthony. *Chippendale Furniture circa 1745–1765*. New York: Clarkson N. Potter, 1968.

*Colton, Henry E. *Mountain Scenery*. . . . Raleigh, North Carolina: W. L. Pomeroy, 1859.

*Cooper, Susan Fenimore. *Wm. West Skiles: A Sketch of Missionary Life at Valle Crucis in Western North Carolina, 1842–1862*. New York: James Pott and Co., 1890.

Cox, Warren E. *Pottery and Porcelain*. 2 vols. New York: Crown Publishers, 1970.

*Crevecoeur, J. Hector St. John. *Letters from an American Farmer*. London: Thomas Davies and Lockyer Davis, 1782.

D'Argenville, Dezallier. *La theorie et la practique du Jardinage*. Chez Pierre Husson, 1711.

*Dayton, Ruth Woods. *Greenbrier Pioneers and Their Homes*. Charleston, WV: West Virginia Publishing Co., 1942.

*Downing, Antoinette, F. and Scully, Vincent J., Jr. *The Architectural Heritage of Newport Rhode Island, 1640–1915*. 2d ed. New York: Bramhall House, 1967.

Downing, Andrew Jackson. *The Architecture of Country Houses*. New York: D. Appleton and Co., 1850.

————. *Cottage Residences*. New York: Wiley and Putnam, 1842. 4th ed. New York: John Wiley, 1852.

————. *Landscape Gardening and Rural Architecture*. New York: Wiley and Putnam, 1841.

*————. *Rural Essays*. New York: Leavitt and Allen, 1858.

*————. *A Treatise on the Theory and Practice of Landscape Gardening, Adapted to North America*. 4th ed. New York: G. P. Putnam, 1849.

*Dwight, Timothy. *Travels in New England and New York*. Barbara M. Solomon, ed. 4 vols. 1821–22. Reprint edition. Cambridge, MA: Harvard University Press, 1969.

Edwards, Paul Francis. *English Garden Ornament*. London: G. Bell, 1965.

Engen, Rodney K. *Randolph Caldecott: "Lord of the Nursery."* London: Oresko Books, 1976.

Fish, Carl Russell. *The Rise of the Common Man*. New York: Macmillan Co., 1927.

Fowler, Orson Squire. *Self-Culture, and the Perfection of Character*. New York: Fowler and Wells, 1853.

*Frazer, Sir James. *The Golden Bough*. New York: Macmillan Co., 1930.

Freud, Sigmund. *On Creativity and the Unconscious*. Selected, with introduction and annotations by Benjamin Nelson: "The 'Uncanny'." New York: Harper and Brothers, 1958.

Friederich, Werner P. *Outline of Comparative Literature*. Chapel Hill: University of North Carolina Press, 1954.

The Gentleman's Magazine. London: 1731–1907.

*Gerard, Alexander. *Essay on Taste*. . . . 3d ed. Edinburgh: 1785.

Geurnet, Jacques. *Daily Life in China on the Eve of the Mongol Invasion: 1250–1276*. H. M. Wright, trans. New York: Macmillan Co., 1962.

*Gilborn, Craig. "Rustic Furniture in the Adirondacks, 1875–1925." The Magazine *Antiques*, June 1976, pp. 1212–1219.

*Gilpin, William. *Three Essays*. 3d ed. London: T. Cadell and W. Davis, 1808.

*————. *An Essay on Prints*. 5th ed. London: A. Strahan, 1802.

Girouard, Mark. *The Victorian Country House*. Oxford: Clarendon Press, 1971.

Gloag, John. *The Englishman's Chair*. London: George Allen and Unwin, 1964.

————. *Victorian Taste*. London: Adam and Charles Black, 1962.

*Goethe, Johann Wolfgang von. *Elective Affinities*. Elizabeth Mayer and Louise Bogan, trans. Chicago: H. Regnery Co., n.d.

Gonzalez-Palacios, Alvar di. *Il mobile nei secoli*. 10 vols. Milan: Fratelli Fabbri Editore, 1969.

*Gothein, Marie Luise. *A History of Garden Art*. 2 vols. Walter P. Wright, ed. London: J. M. Dent and Sons, 1928.

Gombrich, E. H. *Symbolic Images*. London: Phaidon Press, 1972.

Gottshall, Franklin H. *Design for the Craftsman*. Milwaukee: Bruce Publishing Co., 1940.

The Greenbrier Heritage, White Sulphur Springs, West Virginia. Haarlem: Arndt, Preston, Chapin, Lamb and Keen, Inc., n.d.

Hartley, Dorothy. *Made in England*. London: Methuen and Co., n.d.

Hasluck, Paul N. *Rustic Carpentry*. Philadelphia: David McKay, 1907.

*Hauser, Arnold. *The Social History of Art*. 2 vols. New York: Alfred A. Knopf, 1951.

*Hibberd, Shirley. *Rustic Adornments for Homes of Taste*. London: Groombridge and Sons, 1870.

*Hipple, Walter John, Jr. *The Beautiful, the Sublime, and the Picturesque*. Carbondale, IL: Southern Illinois University Press, 1957.

Hogarth, William. *The Analysis of Beauty*. Joseph Burke, ed. Oxford: Clarendon Press, 1955.

*Holt, Elizabeth Gilmore, ed. *A Documentary History of Art*. 2 vols. 2d ed. Garden City, New York: Doubleday, 1957–58.

*Honour, Hugh. *Chinoiserie*. London: John Murray, 1961.

Hopkins, John Henry. *Essay on Gothic Architecture*. Burlington, VT: Smith and Harrington, 1836.

The Horizon Book of the Arts of China. By the editors of *Horizon Magazine*. New York: American Heritage Publishing Co., 1969.

*Hudson, G. F. *Europe and China*. London: Edward Arnold and Co., 1931.

Humphreys, Phebe Westcott. *The Practical Book of Garden Architecture*. Philadelphia: J. B. Lippincott and Co., 1914.

Hunt, W. Ben. *Rustic Construction*. Milwaukee: Bruce Publishing Co., 1939.

*Hunt, John Dixon. "Emblem and Expressionism in the Eighteenth-Century Landscape Garden." *Eighteenth-Century Studies* 4 (Spring 1971).

*Hussey, Christopher. *The Picturesque*. New York: G. P. Putnam, 1927.

Ince, William. *The Universal System of Household Furniture*. London: Ince and Mayhew, 1762.

*Irving, Washington. *The Sketch Book* [1819]. New York: Dodd, Mead and Co. 1954.

*Irving, Washington, Bryant, William Cullen et al. *The Home Book of the Picturesque*. New York: G. P. Putnam, 1852.

*Jackson, F. J. Foakes. *Social Life in England, 1750–1850*. New York: Macmillan Co., 1916.

*James, Henry. *American Scene*. New York: Harper and Brothers, 1907.

*Jefferson, Thomas. *Garden Book*. E. M. Betts, ed. Philadelphia: American Philosophical Society, 1944.

*————. *Notes on the State of Virginia* [1782]. Boston: Walls and Lilly, 1829.

*————. *Writings*. Collected by Paul L. Ford. 12 vols. New York: G. P. Putnam, 1892.

Joyce, Ernest. *The Encyclopedia of Furniture Making*. New York: Drake Publishers, 1970.

The M. and M. Karolik Collection of American Watercolors and Drawings, 1800–1875. 2 vols. Boston: Museum of Fine Arts, 1962.

Kayser, Wolfgang. *The Grotesque in Art and Literature*. Ulrich Weisstein, trans. Bloomington: Indiana University Press, 1963.

Kemp, Edward. *How to Lay Out a Garden or Landscape Gardening*. 2d American ed. New York: Wiley and Halsted, 1858.

Kimball, Fiske. *Thomas Jefferson, Architect*. Boston: Privately printed, 1916.

*Knight, Richard Payne. *An Analytical Inquiry into the Principles of Taste*. 2d ed. London: L. Hansard, 1805.

————. *A Discourse on the Worship of Priapus and Its Connection with the Mystic Theology of the Ancients*. . . . London: Dilettanti Society, n.d

*————. *The Landscape, A Didactic Poem*. London: W. Bulmer and Co., 1794.

*Kris, Ernst. *Psychoanalytic Explorations in Art*. New York: International Universities Press, 1952.

*Lancaster, Clay. "Oriental Forms in American Architecture, 1800–1870." *The Art Bulletin* 29 (September 1947) pp. 183–193.

Langley, Batty. *New Principles of Gardening*. London: A. Bettsworth and J. Battey, 1728.

Le Rouge, G. L. *Détail des nouveaux jardins à la mode*. Paris: Chez Le Rouge, [1776–1787].

*Logan, Frances. *The Old Sweet*. Sweet Springs, WV: Old Sweet Springs, 1940.

*Loudon, John Claudius. *Encyclopedia of Cottage, Farm and Villa Architecture*. London: Longman, Rees, and Orme, 1832.

————. *A Treatise on Farming, Improving and Managing Country Residences*. 2 vols. London: Longman, Hurst, Rees, and Orme, 1806.

Macdonald, Elizabeth Stone. "Preventive Aesthetics." *The House Beautiful* 40 (August 1916), p. 146.

*Manwaring, Elizabeth Wheeler. *Italian Landscape in Eighteenth Century England*. New York: Oxford, 1925.

Manwaring, Robert. *The Cabinet and Chair-maker's Real Friend and Companion*. London: for the author, 1765. Reprint edition. London: J. Tiranti and Co., 1937.

*Marx, Leo. *The Machine in the Garden: Technology and the Pastoral Ideal in America*. New York: Oxford University Press, 1967.

*Masson, Georgina. *Italian Gardens*. London: Thames and Hudson, 1966.

*Mead, Martha Norburn. *Asheville . . . in Land of the Sky*. Richmond, VA: Dietz Press, 1942.

*Minnigerode, Meade. *The Fabulous Forties*. New York: G. P. Putnam, 1924.

*Miller, Perry. *Errand into the Wilderness*: "Nature and the National Ego." Cambridge, MA: Belknap Press, Harvard University Press, 1956.

*Nevins, Allan. *American Social History*. New York: Henry Holt and Co., 1931.

*Nicklin, Philip Holbrook ["Peregrine Prolix"]. *Letters Descriptive of the Virginia Springs. . . .* 2d ed. Philadelphia: H. S. Tanner, 1837.

*Olmstead, Frederick Law. *A Journey in the Back Country*. New York: Mason Brothers, 1860.

*————. *The Walks and Talks of an American Farmer in England*. 2 vols. New York: G. P. Putnam, 1852.

Otto, Celia Jackson. *American Furniture of the Nineteenth Century*. New York: Viking Press, 1965.

The Oxford Book of Eighteenth Century Verse. Chosen by David Nichol Smith. Oxford: Clarendon Press, 1926.

Papworth, John Buonarotti. *Hints on Ornamental Gardening*. London: R. Ackermann, 1823.

Pelton, B. W. *Furniture Making and Cabinet Work*. New York: D. Van Nostrand Co., 1949.

A Picturesque Promenade Round Dorking, in Surrey. London: John Warren, 1822.

Polo, Marco. *Travels*. New York: Horace Liveright, 1926.

*Pope, Alexander. *Complete Poetical Works*. Boston: Houghton Mifflin Co., 1903.

Price, R. G. G. *A History of Punch*. London: Wm. Collins Sons and Co., 1957.

*Price, Sir Uvedale, bart. *Essays on the Picturesque, as Compared with the Sublime and the Beautiful. . . .* London: J. Mawman, 1810.

*————. *A Letter to H. Repton, Esq. . . .* London: J. Tobson, 1795.

Pugin, Augustus Charles. *Modern Furniture*. London: M. A. Nattali, n.d.

Pugin, A. W. N. *Gothic Furniture in the Style of the XV Century*. London: Ackermann and Co., 1835.

*Rand, Benjamin, ed. *The Life, Unpublished Letters, and Philosophical Regimen of Anthony, Earl of Shaftesbury. . . .* New York: Macmillan Co., 1900.

Rand, Edward Sprague, Jr. *Flowers for the Parlor and Garden*. Boston: J. E. Tilton and Co., 1863.

*Reed, Amy Louise. *The Background of Gray's Elegy*. New York: Columbia University Press, 1924.

Reich, Annie. "The Structure of the Grotesque-Comic Sublimation." *Bulletin of the Menninger Clinic* 13 (1949) pp. 160–171.

*Repton, Humphry. *The Landscape Gardening and Landscape Architecture of the Late Humphry Repton, Esq. . . .* J. C. Loudon, ed. London: Longman and Co., 1840.

Rheims, Maurice. *The Flowering of Art Nouveau*. New York: Harry N. Abrams, 1966.

*Roper, Laura Wood. *Frederick Law Olmsted*. Baltimore: Johns Hopkins University Press, 1973.

Rowland, Daniel B. *Mannerism—Style and Mood*. New Haven: Yale University Press, 1964.

*Ruskin, John. *Works*. E. T. Cook and Alexander Wedderburn, eds. 39 vols. New York: Longmans Green and Co., 1903–12.

Saunders, Richard. *Collecting and Restoring Wicker Furniture*. New York: Crown Publishers, 1976.

*Schmitt, J. Peter. *Back to Nature*. New York: Oxford University Press, 1969.

*Schuyler, David P. "Rural Values and Urban America: The Social Thought of Andrew Jackson Downing." M.A. thesis, University of North Carolina, 1976.

*Scully, Vincent. "Romantic Rationalism and the Expression of Structure in Wood: Downing, Wheeler, Gardner, and the 'Stick Style', 1840–1876." *Art Bulletin* 25 (June 1953) pp. 121–142.

*Sirén, Osvald. *China and the Gardens of Europe of the Eighteenth Century*. New York: Ronald Press Co., 1950.

*Steegman, John. *Victorian Taste*. Cambridge, MA: MIT Press, 1971.

*Stenerson, Douglas C. "Emerson and the Agrarian Tradition." *Journal of the History of Ideas* 14 (January 1953) pp. 95–115.

Stephenson, Sue H. *Basketry of the Appalachian Mountains*. New York: Van Nostrand Reinhold Co., 1977.

Symonds, John Addington. *The Renaissance in Italy* 3 vols. London: John Murray, 1921.

Upjohn, Richard. *Rural Architecture*. New York: G. P. Putnam, 1852.

Van Rensselaer, Mrs. Schuyler. *Art Out-of-Doors*. New York: Charles Scribner's Sons, 1893.

*Vasari, Giorgio. *Lives of the Painters, Sculptors, and Architects*. 4 vols. London: J. M. Dent and Sons, n.d.

Vaux, Calvert. *Villas and Cottages*. New York: Harper and Brothers, 1857.

Vitruvius, Pollio. *Vitruvii de architectura libri decem (iterum edidit Valentinus Rose)*. Bibliotheca scriptorum Graecorum et Romanorum Teubneriana, D. Lipsiae, teubner, 1899.

Vitruvius. *de Architectura, The Ten Books on Architecture*. Cambridge, MA: Harvard University Press, 1914.

*Von Erdberg, Eleanor. *Chinese Influences on European Garden Structures*. Cambridge, MA: Harvard University Press, 1936.

Wainwright, Nicholas B., ed. *A Philadelphia Perspective, the Diary of Sidney George Fisher Covering the Years 1834–1871*. Philadelphia: Historical Society of Pennsylvania, 1967.

*Walpole, Horace, Earl of Orford. *The Letters of Horace Walpole*. Peter Cunningham, ed. 9 vols. Edinburgh: John Grant, 1906.

*————. *Notes to a New Edition of Thomas Whately and Observations on Modern Gardening*. London: 1801.

Waterman, Thomas Tileston. *The Mansions of Virginia 1706–1776*. New York: Bonanza Books, 1945.

Weaver, Lawrence. *Small Country Houses*. London: Country Life, 1914.

Wheeler, Gervaise. *Rural Homes*. New York: Charles Scribner's Sons, 1851.

The World. London, 1753–1756.

Worringer, W. *Form Problems of the Gothic*. New York: G. E. Stechert and Co., 1912.

Wright, G. N., Rev. *China in a Series of Views Displaying the Scenery, Architecture, and Social Habits of that Ancient Empire*. London: M. A. Fisher and Son, 1843.

*Wörtenberger, Franzsepp. *Mannerism*. Michael Heron, trans. New York: Holt, Rinehart and Winston, 1963.

Index

Manwaring, Robert, 8, 26, 28, *29*, 31, 79
measurement, 85, 91
Medici, Catherine de', 20
medievalism, revival of, 51
Meissen porcelain, 17
Middle Ages, hermitage, 20
Miles Brewton house, 38
Ming porcelain, 16
Monticello, 38
Moorman, J. J., 52
morality, grotto, 22
mortise-and-tendon joints, 86
Museo Civico (Belluno), 26

nails, 87
Nation, The (magazine), 49
Nature
    hermitage, 23
    romantic view of, 40
    rustic furniture, 23
    Victorians, 49, 50
neoclassical style, 38
    England, 35
    Georgian, 38
    revival in, 10
    grotto, 22
neo-Gothic style, England, 9
Nero, 18
Newport (RI), 41
Newman, John Henry, 42

oak (white), 57, 60
Old Hickory Chair Company, 57
"Old White" hotel, 52
Olmsted, Frederick Law, 46, 49, 50
Oriental art, 18
    rococo style, 16
    see also entries under China; Chinoiserie
Origin of Species (Darwin), 51
Orleans, duke of, 9
Over, Charles, 26, 35, *36*, *37*
Oxford Reform Movement, 42

paint, 93
painting
    arabesque, 18
    Hudson River school, 38
    landscape gardening, 14, 16
    serpentine line, 15
Palissy, Bernard, 20
Palladian tradition, 16
Pan, 20
parks (city), Downing, 46
Parodi, Filippo, 26
parterre, Italian, 50
Partridge, William, 26
Paxton, Joseph, 49
Pembroke, earl of, 21
pergolas, construction of, 108
Philip II (king of Spain), 20
picturesque
    condemned, 50
    Downing, 43–47
    Flat Rock (NC), 41
    furniture, 47
    Jefferson, 40
    Virginia Springs, 40
pitcher
    Appalachian rustic, 68
    grotesque, *69*
plantation estate, American south, 38
Pompeii, excavation of, 10
Pope, Alexander, 14

posture, chair design, 91
Poussin, Nicholas and Gaspar, 14
Priapus, 17, 20
proportion, design, 92–93
Protestantism, 17
psychology, Renaissance, 20
Punch (magazine), 47–48, 67

Quinn, Joseph Clarence, 54

Raphael, 18
Reid, James, 38
Renaissance
    classicism, 9
    Domus Aurea excavation, 18
    hermitage, 20
resorts, 19th century, 50–51
Restoration (English), style, 9
rhododendron wood, 55, 67, 68
Robertson, Thomas B., 58
Robinson Crusoe (Defoe), 27
rocking chair, *56*
rococo-Gothic, England, 35
rococo style
    Chinoiserie, 16, 30
    Chippendale, 32
    France, 9
    revival in, 49
Roman Catholicism, 42
Romano, Guilio, 18
romantic movement, rustic revival, 74
Rome (ancient), 9, 10, 18
romantic view, style, 10
Rosa, Salvator, 14, 16
Rousseau, J. J., 10
root chairs, *25*, *31*, 88
root furniture, 27, 28
    Appalachian rustic, 55
    origins, 30
roots, bending of, 80–81,
Ruskin, John, 18, 35, 36, 49
rustic, definition of, 8
rustic furniture
    grotesque, 23
    revival in, 53
rustic style, English gardens, 17
Rustic Adornments for Homes of Taste
    (Hibberd), 49

Saratoga Springs (NY), 41
sassafras wood, 68
Scott, Sir Walter, 35
seasoning, of wood, 79–80
seat weaving, 94–95
Seminole Indians, 60
serpentine line, 15, 16
settee(s), *27*, *29*, *32*, *44*, *48*, *54*, *55*, *59*, 65,
    72, 102–104
Shaftesbury, earl of, 10
Shakers, 74
Shakespeare, William, 9, 15
shelters, see structures
Shenstone, William, 34
sideboard, *66*
Skiles, William West, 42
smoking table, *70*
Southey, Robert, 34–35
Spanish steamer chair, *59*
Steegman, John, 48
Stones of Venice, The (Ruskin), 49
straw, for thatching, 109
structures
    English gardens, 16–17
    garden "conceits," 14

style
    attitudes and, 10
    psychology of, 9–10
    social sources of, 10–11
Stylites, Saint Simon, 20
suburb, creation of, 44
summerhouse, *44*, *45*, *47*, *73*, 111
    construction of, 108–109
    plans for, 111–114
    Hibberd's, 50
Swiss chalet, 38, 70, 72
Swisswork, 89

tables
    Appalachian rustic, 66–70
    bases for, *68*
    corduroy, pattern for, 99
    design, 92
    Gothic, *67*
    tops for, 89, *99*
thatching, 109–110
Thonet, Michael, *60*
tools, rustic furniture, 78
topia, 18, *19*
tourist, 34, 52
Tragic Mansions (Lydig), 52
trees
    Eastern attitudes, 28
    pruning of, 81
tripod tables, *69*, *70*
*True Recipe, A, by which all Frenchmen may
    learn to add to their treasures* (Palissy), 20
Tucker, Anna Washington, 51
Tudor bed, *119*
Tuilleries garden, 20

uncanny, grotesque, 20
University of Virginia, 38
Upjohn, Richard, 47

Valle Crucis Abbey, 41–42
van der Rohe, Mies, 23
varnish, 93
Vaux, Calvert, 43, 46
Venus, 17
Victorian chair, *50*
Victorian era, England, 47–50
Victorian Taste (Steegman), 48
Villa d'Este (Tivoli), 17
vine-covered cottage, invention of, 36–38
Virginia Springs, 40–41
*Virginia Springs and Springs of the South and
    West, The* (Moorman), 52
Vitruvius, 18

Wallace, Wm. Ross, 51
Walpole, Horace, 14, 35
weaving, *59*, 94–95
White Sulphur Springs (WV), 41
wicker furniture, 50–51
wickerwork chair, 27
wilderness, escape to, 51–52
willow, basketwork furniture, 57
willow chair, *61*, *64*, *100*
Wilton House, 21
Windsor captain's chairs, 56
Windsor chair, 27, 52
Woburn Abbey, grotto at, 21
women, idealization of, 51
wood
    bending of, 80–85
    choice of, 79
    cutting and seasoning of, 79–80
Wren, Sir Christopher, 35
Wrighte, William, 26, 60